THE DEAD GOOD DADGAD BOOK

Phil Mathison

Published by DEADGOOD Publications
East Yorkshire HU15 2RF, England
©2004

Second Edition 2007

Preface to the Second Edition of the
DEAD GOOD DADGAD Book

Welcome to the second edition of the DEAD GOOD DADGAD Book. We hope that within its pages you'll find help and inspiration for years to come. The book contains over 200 frequently used chord diagrams in this tuning. It does not claim to be an exhaustive list, just a dead good starting point for your adventures in this great tuning!

The assumption has been made by the author that someone using the book has some knowledge of the guitar already. As DADGAD is a different tuning from the normal EADGBE, it is obvious that all the chord shapes will be different. To a novice, the guitar is demanding enough, without having to learn an alternate set of chords! Furthermore, the techniques learned on a normally tuned guitar will, in time, be carried across to the D modal tuning to very good effect.

On the other hand, the book is not intended to be THE definitive work on the tuning, or the last word on it. Rather, it is a useful resource and reference work, to be consulted as you develop familiarity with the tuning.

The author has used the DADGAD (or D modal) tuning to great effect for a number of years, and can recommend it to any guitarist brave enough (or mad enough!) to experiment with its possibilities. So get in there and have a dead good time!

Incidentally, chords listed in this book as add9 (no 3rd) are more usually described in modern terms as sus2. That is, the ninth note of the scale is added, but the chord does not have the third note of the scale. Therefore, the chord is atonal ie. neither major nor minor. However, I'm a bit old fashioned - there was no such thing as a sus2 when I was nobbut a lad!

Also available from the same author:
THE DEAD GOOD WACKY CHORD BOOK
(The chords they don't want you to know)
ISBN 0-9546937-2-8
Published by DEADGOOD Publications
East Yorkshire HU15 2RF, England
©2005

*Nearly 200 interesting chords to spice up your playing,
not normally found in most available chord books.*

Contents

D Modal Tuning – An Introduction

D Modal, or DADGAD tuning, is one of many alternative tunings available to the guitarist. It is popular with folk musicians, but can be found in other genres as well.

The normal guitar tuning is E,A,D,G,B,E, across the instrument from the sixth string (the thickest) to the first string. As the nickname for this tuning implies, the strings are tuned D,A,D,G,A,D, in order from the thickest string. If all the open strings are played, a D sus4 chord is generated.

It is obviously apparent that the tuning is designed to work to the maximum effect in the key of D, but it can also be used in the key of G, and to a lesser extent in the key of F (D minor).

The richness of its sound lies in two main areas.

Firstly, the strength of the basic D and A chord sounds, which have no third note i.e. in modern parlance, they are D5 and A5 chords i.e. power chords. The third note in the scale tends to weaken the sound and generate the tonality of the work. Therefore, the omission of the F# note within the basic D chord, and the omission of the C# note in the basic A chord, create powerful cornerstones to the tuning's potential on the tonic and dominant chords.

Secondly, the beauty of this modal sound is the added notes that can be positioned in relatively basic chords to enrich the texture of the music. They also extend the chord, creating new possibilities, Therefore, it is undesirable in this tuning to try and blindly clone standard chords from normal tuning. To do so, one negates the benefits of this alternative mode i.e. the guitar will tend to sound fairly similar if the same notes are being voiced.

The chord section of the book is divided into headings under each root (or tonic) note on which the chord is formed. Therefore, you will see headings for the following notes; A, A#/Bb, B, C, D, E, F, F#/Gb and G, in that order. As the mode has some limitations, there will be no headings for D#/Eb, G#/Ab or C#/Db, as these are difficult to play, and unlikely to be used in this mode. If chords on these notes are required, then it is likely that the key will require a capo. This will facilitate the keys in which these chords are likely to be found. Look under the section entitled 'Capo Chord Possibilities' for help.

Generally, the illustrations will give a number of permutations for each chord, so that you can explore the variety that this tuning affords. Even on the basic three chords of D, G and A, there are a wide variety of permutations, all with their own particular sound - so experiment!

Advantages

This tuning has a number of advantages for a guitarist.

Firstly, it gives an alternate tuning to the standard one, and so a wider range of voicings for the instrument.

Secondly, it is a singer's tuning, for the resonance of the chords produced tends to enrich and support the vocal.

Thirdly, the tuning gives strong and colourful backing on only a handful of chords, based around the tonic chord (D), the sub-dominant (G) and the dominant (A). As many songs are based on or around this 'three chord trick', then this tuning gives a powerful backing for the singer.

Fourthly, many of the chord positions offer ample opportunity to add notes that give the tuning its character.

Fifthly, the 6th and 4th strings producing a D drone, albeit an octave apart, can create an ideal accompaniment. This is particularly true in Celtic music.

Finally, as the basic chord position starts with just a one finger stopping (see diagram D1), barring this can generate other chords. For example, the basic chord barred to the first fret will generate an E♭ chord. It will be a power chord, which is neither major nor minor. This may be appropriate to the song, but if the tonality of the major or minor is required, it can then become a disadvantage.

As we shall see in the next section, there are also disadvantages to the DADGAD tuning.

Disadvantages

Just as we have seen that the tuning has advantages for the guitarist, so it also has some disadvantages.

Firstly, to play in a variety of keys, much capo work is required. Some keys can be difficult to obtain because the capo is needed too far up the guitar neck.

Secondly, because three of the strings are dropped, or lower than normal tuning, it is very easy to bend them out of tune. The greater amount of capo work also tends to exaggerate this, as anyone who has used a capo will know!

Thirdly, modulation, or key-changing within a song is much more difficult than with normal tuning. If the song starts in the key of D, a change to the key of say, E, in the middle will probably be out of the question. At the very least, the basic chord positions that existed in the earlier part of the song will probably be unplayable, even if barre chords are used.

Fourthly, simply barring does not provide the range of possibilities available in normal tuning. Obtaining a range of major chords in different keys can be particularly challenging.

Finally, it can be difficult to obtain some chords without added notes being included. It is all part of the tuning's character!

Some progressions to get you started

Below are a list of DADGAD chord progressions to get you started. Call them a taster of the sound of the tuning. You can tell at a glance the basic root chords to be used, but the numbers allude to the chord diagram, i.e. D20 isn't a magical new chord, but actually a D7 chord with a D20 diagram number.

The numbers in the circles on the chord diagrams refer to the finger to be used, i.e. ① refers to the first, or index finger, and ④ refers to the little finger. Open strings that can be played are marked by an empty circle at the nut, but don't play strings that have a cross in the circle. Optional fingerings are displayed with a finger number inside a diamond.

You can obviously play the sequences strummed or picked, it depends how you feel. I have included a separate chapter called 'Picked progressions', that give you some chords I think show the beauty of the tuning when picked.

Likewise, they can be played slow or fast, in common time, waltz, two step or compound time. It's up to you. The object is to get you started, and for you to listen to the subtle (and not so subtle) differences that this tuning offers the guitarist.

Furthermore, don't be scared to add a finger, or miss one off on the chord shapes. Some possibilities will sound dissonant, but you may well discover little gems hidden away within this great tuning. Enjoy!

1)	D1	G5	A1			
2)	D9	E10	G16	A15		
3)	D7	B12	G13	A16	A1	
4)	D5	A8	B16	A26	G5	A3
5)	D6	E9	D10	G14	A2	
6)	D2	G19	G5	C2		
7)	D31	D10	G3	E4	A19	
8)	D1	A39	C4	G5		
9)	D42	C12	B♭6	A36		

Progressions (continued)

10)	D43	C11	F3	G2	A13	
11)	D53	B♭4	F1	C10		
12)	D48	G24	B♭5	A14		
13)	G7	A32	G4	C13	D37	D7
14)	G1	D10	E11	C9	D41	
15)	G5	E8	C4	D3		
16)	G10	B14	C14	E7	D38	D9
17)	G30	F3	C9	D24	D21	
18)	G24	B♭9	C2	F5	C12	
19)	A1	D1	F#4	E3		
20)	A5	G13	D10	G1		
21)	A4	B17	A3	D9	E1	
22)	A7	G4	C5	D5		
23)	A30	G13	D10	G14		
24)	A38	G4	C7	E1	D1	
25)	A31	G20	F2	G2		
26)	A34	D43	E4			
27)	B15	A27	G22	A28		
28)	B9	A8	D7	E9	G1	
29)	E11	D40	C14	D2		
30)	E7	F#5	G3	B12	A2	

Picked progressions

The sound of the following progressions will illustrate better than words the beauty of this tuning. The numbers in brackets tell you which string to use as the bass note.

As explained in the chapter 'Some progressions to get you started', the numbers allude to the chord diagram, i.e. B17 is not some weird, unheard of chord, but a B minor added9th chord with B17 as its diagram number.

1)	B15 (5)	A27 (5)	G22 (6)	A27 (5)	
2)	D40 (6)	G10 (5)	E10 (6)	A22 (5)	
3)	D7 (4) Optional finger not used			A8 (6)	G4 (6) A6 (5)
4)	A39 (5)	G20 (4)	D6 (6)	C10 (5)	
5)	D1 (6)	E9 (6)	D10 (6)	G13 (6)	B11 (5) A1 (5)
6)	G16 (6)	D21 (6)	E11 (6)	C14 (5)	
7)	D42 (5)	C10 (5)	B^{b}4 (5)	A36 (5)	
8)	G13 (6)	D10 (6)	C6 (6)	E9 (6)	D1 (6)
9)	D45 (6)	F3 (6)	C9 (6)	G3 (6)	
10)	D44 (6)	G30 (6)	B^{b}6 (6)	A28 (5)	

The Drone sound

A major characteristic of the DADGAD tuning is the drone quality that is inherent in the 4th and 6th strings being tuned to a D, albeit an octave apart. To give you a sample of the drone sound, here is a list of progressions to get you started.

To keep the sound, it is essential that you ignore instructions in any of the chord diagrams below NOT to play the 6th string. The 6th string will always be open to generate the drone. Now try the following chord progressions, remembering to keep that 6th string droning away!

1)	D9	G2	A6	
2)	D2	A3	G14	
3)	D7	A37	G7	
4)	D1	G19	G5	
5)	D3	C2	G16 (no 1st finger on the 6th string)	
6)	D2	D36	G5	
7)	D7	A7	G7	A7
8)	D42	C10	G25	C10
9)	D43	A31	Bb4	C12
10)	D46	D35	G7	

Ornamentation

D Modal tuning lends itself to some very effective ornamentation over the basic chords. Introducing grace notes adds interest to a song, and is sure to impress your friends!

A little word here on keys. If we are adding grace notes to our work, we need to know that they are the <u>right</u> grace notes! As stated elsewhere, the tuning is primarily for the key of D, which contains the notes of D, E, F#, G, A, B and C#. In chord terms, that means D major, E minor, F# minor, G major, A major and B minor are used.

The key of G contains G, A, B, C, D, E and F#, which will be found in the following chords: G major, A minor, B minor, C major, D major and E minor.

The key of F, which is mainly used in this tuning by the playing of D minor, contains the notes F, G, A, B♭, C, D and E. This gives us the chords F major, G minor, A minor, B♭ major, C major and D minor.

Page 16 has a diagram showing the notes on the neck of the guitar in this tuning, so if there is any doubt about which sequence to use, check which key you are in with the above lists.

We'll deal first with the key of D. The letter in the brackets refers to the notes being sounded at each position. See pages 90 and 91 for diagrams.

Phrase 1A

Place the 1st finger on fret 2 of the 1st string (E), and then hammer the 4th finger onto the 4th fret of the 1st string (F#). Pull the 4th finger off, and roll through the 1st finger (E) and onto the open string (D). There are now three ways to end the sequence.

    i)   On the chords D, G and Bm, finish on this open D note.

    ii)   On A and Em, finish by hammering the 1st finger on the 2nd fret of the 1st string (E).

    iii)   After the open 1st string played above, sound the open 2nd string and then the open 3rd string. Finish with the 3rd finger on the 4th fret of the 4th string (F#). This ending sounds great on a D major chord.

All three versions can also be played in the key of G as well. The ornamentation in versions i) and ii) can also be played an octave down, by starting on the 4th string, not the 1st. However, it can't be done for version iii), as you'd run out of strings!

Phrase 1B

Hammer the 1st finger on fret 2 of the 1st string (E), then pull off to the open string (D). Now hammer on the 4th finger onto the 4th fret of the 2nd string (C#). On D, G or Bm chords, finish on the open 1st string (D). On A or Em, finish by hammering the 1st finger on the 2nd fret of the 1st string (E). This ornamentation can also be played an octave down, by starting on the 4th string, not the 1st.

Phrase 1C

Start by placing the 1st finger on fret 2 of the 3rd string (A). Now use the 4th finger to hammer the 4th fret of the 3rd string (B). Pull the 4th finger off, and roll through the 1st finger (A) and onto the open string (G). Finish by returning the 1st finger to the 2nd fret of the 3rd string (A). This little run works particularly well on D major and A major.

Now let's look at embellishing chords in other keys.

Phrase 2A

Place the 1st finger on the 2nd fret of the 1st string (E), then hammer the 2nd finger onto the 3rd fret of the 1st string (F). Now pull off the 2nd finger, roll through the 1st finger (E), and onto the open string (D). You can finish here, or you can continue, by hammering the 2nd finger onto the 3rd fret of the 2nd string (C), and finish on the open 1st string (D). This will sound great over a D minor chord. These grace notes are in the key of F. Again, this ornamentation can also be played an octave down, by starting on the 4th string, not the 1st.

Phrase 2B

Hammer the 1st finger on fret 2 of the 1st string (E), then pull off to the open string (D). Now hammer the 2nd finger onto the 3rd fret of the 2nd string (C). On a D minor chord, finish on the open 1st string (D). On a C or Am, finish by hammering the 1st finger on the 2nd fret of the 1st string (E). This little run works in either the key of C or the key of F. This phrasing can also be played an octave down, by starting on the 4th string, not the 1st.

These are just a few of the many embellishments possible in this tuning.

If you want to play the final note in the phrases as part of a chord, then the finger used may vary from the above descriptions. For instance, in Phrase 1C, the 1st finger will be fine if you land on the D chord in Diagram D1, but if you land on the A chord in diagram A1, the 3rd finger will be the appropriate one for this chord shape.

The Order of chords

Within each root note section, i.e. D, A, C etc, the order of the chords is approximately as follows:

5th (no 3rd)
Major
6th
6/9
Major 7th
7th
7th sus 4th
Major 9th
9th
Added 9th
11th
Sus 4th
Added 4th

Minor
Minor 6th
Minor 7th
Minor 9th
Minor add 9th
Minor 11th

There are slight variations on this order, as some root notes have many possible chords, i.e. D, G and A. Other notes, such as F#, have only limited possibilities, and so many of the chord permutations listed above will not be shown.

The chords shown in the book do not claim to be an exhaustive list of the possibilities in the tuning. However, they are a good start. If in any doubt, use the diagrams as your starting point, and then experiment and improvise. Part of the pleasure of learning a new tuning is to explore its potential for yourself. It is a journey of discovery, and though the chords may be familiar to someone who has worked with DADGAD for a while, their power and beauty will, hopefully, be refreshing for the novice.

Capo Chord Possibilities

To use the tuning in a variety of keys, a capo is essential. Most singers have favourite keys, but at some stage they will inevitably require the ability to raise or lower the pitch, in order to accommodate their vocal range comfortably.

Some background here will help you identify chords when you start to capo-up the guitar in DADGAD tuning.

The chord charts in this book will show you shapes for chords on the following root (or tonic) notes ; D, E, F, F#/ G♭, G, A, A#/ B♭, B and C.

The chart below shows you what these chords become when you capo-up the chord shapes illustrated in the charts. Only the chords generated up to fret 9 are listed, as some chord positions in the book will become impractical as the capo moves up the guitar neck, being too high to play. Just chose another shape!

OPEN	D	E	F	F#/G♭	G	A	A#/B♭	B	C
FRET 1	D#/E♭	F	F#/G♭	G	G#/A♭	A#/B♭	B	C	C#/D♭
FRET 2	E	F#/G♭	G	G#/A♭	A	B	C	C#/D♭	D
FRET 3	F	G	G#/A♭	A	A#/B♭	C	C#/D♭	D	D#/E♭
FRET 4	F#/G♭	G#/A♭	A	A#/B♭	B	C#/D♭	D	D#/E♭	E
FRET 5	G	A	A#/B♭	B	C	D	D#/E♭	E	F
FRET 6	G#/A♭	A#/B♭	B	C	C#/D♭	D#/E♭	E	F	F#/G♭
FRET 7	A	B	C	C#/D♭	D	E	F	F#/G♭	G
FRET 8	A#/B♭	C	C#/D♭	D	D#/E♭	F	F#/G♭	G	G#/A♭
FRET 9	B	C#/D♭	D	D#/E♭	E	F#/G♭	G	G#/A♭	A

Major Standard Positions

On page 86 you will see three possible chord shapes for creating MAJOR chords anywhere along the guitar neck. Some of these shapes will be duplicated in the main body of chord shapes preceding this page, but many will not. As stated in the introduction, I do not recommend slavishly following standard chords in this tuning, but should you need them at any time, here they are! Remember the enharmonic notes i.e C$^\#$ is also D^b, D$^\#$ is E^b, F$^\#$ is G^b, G$^\#$ is A^b, and A$^\#$ is B^b, depending on the key signature.

The first chord listed is the one produced when the shape illustrated on page 86 is played. The chords created as you move up the neck are then listed, fret by fret. The first column below represents the left hand diagram, the second column below represents the middle diagram, and the third column below represents the right hand diagram. The fret number refers to the position of the FIRST finger.

Major 1		Major 2		Major 3	
Fret 1	E Major	Fret 1	E Major	Fret 1	A^{b}Major
Fret 2	F Major	Fret 2	F Major	Fret 2	A Major
Fret 3	F$^\#$Major	Fret 3	F$^\#$Major	Fret 3	B^{b}Major
Fret 4	G Major	Fret 4	G Major	Fret 4	B Major
Fret 5	A^{b}Major	Fret 5	A^{b}Major	Fret 5	C Major
Fret 6	A Major	Fret 6	A Major	Fret 6	D^{b}Major
Fret 7	B^{b}Major	Fret 7	B^{b}Major	Fret 7	D Major
Fret 8	B Major	Fret 8	B Major	Fret 8	E^{b}Major
Fret 9	C Major	Fret 9	C Major	Fret 9	E Major
Fret 10	D^{b}Major	Fret 10	D^{b}Major	Fret 10	F Major
Fret 11	D Major	Fret 11	D Major	Fret 11	F$^\#$Major
Fret 12	E^{b}Major	Fret 12	E^{b}Major	Fret 12	G Major

Minor Standard Positions

On page 87 you will see three possible chord shapes for creating MINOR chords anywhere along the guitar neck. Some of these shapes will be duplicated in the main body of chord shapes preceding this page, but many will not. As stated in the introduction, I do not recommend slavishly following standard chords in this tuning, but should you need them at any time, here they are! Remember the enharmonic notes i.e $C^\#$ is also D^b, $D^\#$ is E^b, $F^\#$ is G^b, $G^\#$ is A^b, and $A^\#$ is B^b, depending on the key signature.

The first chord listed is the one produced when the shape illustrated on page 87 is played. The chords created as you move up the neck are then listed, fret by fret. The first column below represents the left hand diagram, the second column below represents the middle diagram, and the third column below represents the right hand diagram. The fret number refers to the position of the FIRST finger.

Minor 1		Minor 2		Minor 3	
Fret 1	F Minor	Fret 1	F Minor	Fret 1	E♭Minor
Fret 2	F#Minor	Fret 2	F#Minor	Fret 2	E Minor
Fret 3	G Minor	Fret 3	G Minor	Fret 3	F Minor
Fret 4	G#Minor	Fret 4	G#Minor	Fret 4	F#Minor
Fret 5	A Minor	Fret 5	A Minor	Fret 5	G Minor
Fret 6	B♭Minor	Fret 6	B♭Minor	Fret 6	G#Minor
Fret 7	B Minor	Fret 7	B Minor	Fret 7	A Minor
Fret 8	C Minor	Fret 8	C Minor	Fret 8	B♭Minor
Fret 9	C#Minor	Fret 9	C#Minor	Fret 9	B Minor
Fret 10	D Minor	Fret 10	D Minor	Fret 10	C Minor
Fret 11	E♭Minor	Fret 11	E♭Minor	Fret 11	C#Minor
Fret 12	E Minor	Fret 12	E Minor	Fret 12	D Minor

More Positions 1

On page 88 you will see three possible chord shapes for creating firstly, 5ths (power chords), then Added 9ths (no 3rd), and finally Major chords with added 9ths, anywhere along the guitar neck. Some of these shapes will be duplicated in the main body of chord shapes preceding this page, but many will not. Remember the enharmonic notes i.e C# is also D♭, D# is E♭, F# is G♭, G# is A♭, and A# is B♭, depending on the key signature.

The first chord listed is the one produced when the shape illustrated on page 88 is played. The chords created as you move up the neck are then listed, fret by fret. The first column below represents the left hand diagram, the second column below represents the middle diagram, and the third column below represents the right hand diagram. The fret number refers to the position of the FIRST finger.

5th (no 3rd)		Add9 (no 3rd)		Major add9	
Fret 1	E♭5	Fret 1	E♭ add9 (no 3rd)	Fret 1	A♭ add9
Fret 2	E5	Fret 2	E add9 (no 3rd)	Fret 2	A add9
Fret 3	F5	Fret 3	F add9 (no 3rd)	Fret 3	B♭ add9
Fret 4	F#5	Fret 4	F# add9 (no 3rd)	Fret 4	B add9
Fret 5	G5	Fret 5	G add9 (no 3rd)	Fret 5	C add9
Fret 6	A♭5	Fret 6	A♭ add9 (no 3rd)	Fret 6	D♭ add9
Fret 7	A5	Fret 7	A add9 (no 3rd)	Fret 7	D add9
Fret 8	B♭5	Fret 8	B♭ add9 (no 3rd)	Fret 8	E♭ add9
Fret 9	B5	Fret 9	B add9 (no 3rd)	Fret 9	E add9
Fret 10	C5	Fret 10	C add9 (no 3rd)	Fret 10	F add9
Fret 11	D♭5	Fret 11	D♭ add9 (no 3rd)	Fret 11	F# add9
Fret 12	D5	Fret 12	D add9 (no 3rd)	Fret 12	G add9

More Positions 2

On page 89 you will see three more chord shapes for creating firstly, suspended 4ths, then 7ths (no 3rd), and finally 7th suspended 4ths chords, anywhere along the guitar neck. Some of these shapes will be duplicated in the main body of chord shapes preceding this page, but many will not. Remember the enharmonic notes i.e C# is also Db, D# is Eb, F# is Gb, G# is Ab, and A# is Bb, depending on the key signature.

The first chord listed is the one produced when the shape illustrated on page 89 is played. The chords created as you move up the neck are then listed, fret by fret. The first column below represents the left hand diagram, the second column below represents the middle diagram, and the third column below represents the right hand diagram. The fret number refers to the position of the FIRST finger.

Sus4th		7th (no 3rd)		7th sus4	
Fret 1	Eb sus4	Fret 1	Bb7 (no 3)	Fret 1	Bb7 sus4
Fret 2	E sus4	Fret 2	B7 (no 3)	Fret 2	B7 sus4
Fret 3	F sus4	Fret 3	C7 (no 3)	Fret 3	C7 sus4
Fret 4	F# sus4	Fret 4	Db7 (no 3)	Fret 4	Db7 sus4
Fret 5	G sus4	Fret 5	D7 (no 3)	Fret 5	D7 sus4
Fret 6	Ab sus4	Fret 6	Eb7 (no 3)	Fret 6	Eb7 sus4
Fret 7	A sus4	Fret 7	E7 (no 3)	Fret 7	E7 sus4
Fret 8	Bb sus4	Fret 8	F7 (no 3)	Fret 8	F7 sus4
Fret 9	B sus4	Fret 9	F#7 (no 3)	Fret 9	F#7 sus4
Fret 10	C sus4	Fret 10	G7 (no 3)	Fret 10	G7 sus4
Fret 11	Db sus4	Fret 11	Ab7 (no 3)	Fret 11	Ab7 sus4
Fret 12	D sus4	Fret 12	A7 (no 3)	Fret 12	A7 sus4

Notes On Guitar Neck - D Modal Tuning

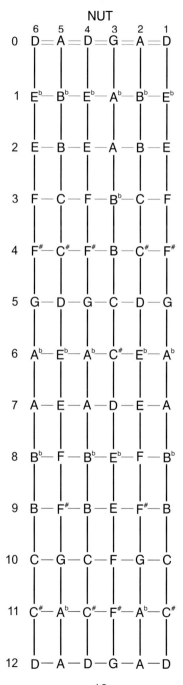

Chords in DADGAD Tuning

Key: ◯ Hold down the string at this fret   ⊗ Don't play this string   ◇ Optional fingering

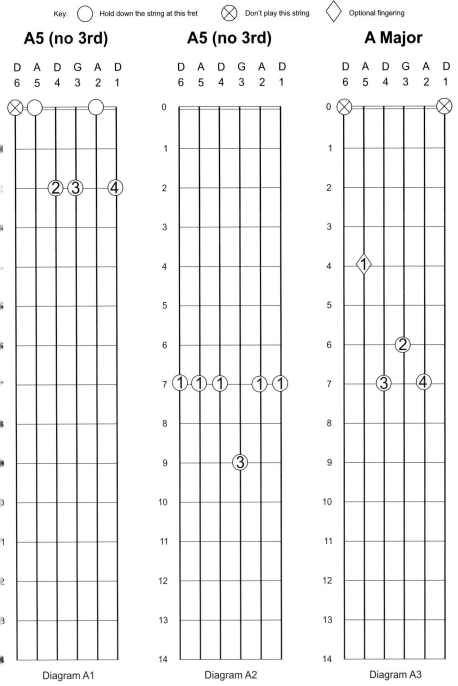

A5 (no 3rd)
Diagram A1

A5 (no 3rd)
Diagram A2

A Major
Diagram A3

17

Chords in DADGAD Tuning

Key: ◯ Hold down the string at this fret   ⊗ Don't play this string   ◇ Optional fingering

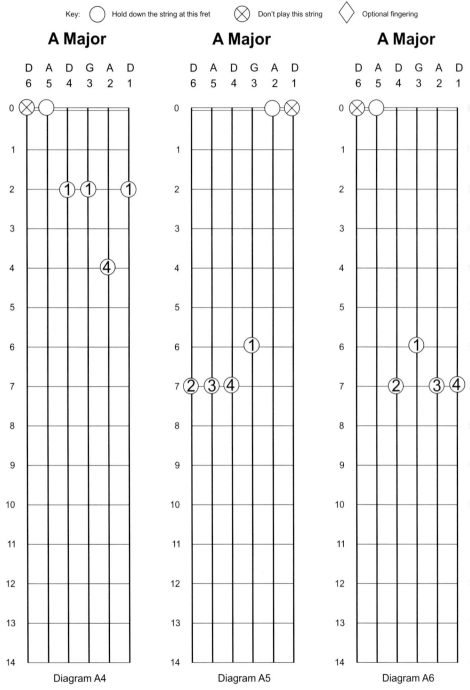

Diagram A4

Diagram A5

Diagram A6

18

Chords in DADGAD Tuning

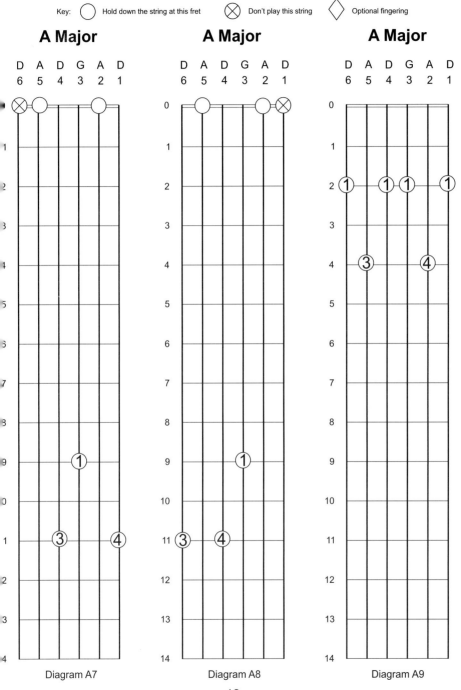

A Major

D A D G A D
6 5 4 3 2 1

Diagram A7

A Major

D A D G A D
6 5 4 3 2 1

Diagram A8

A Major

D A D G A D
6 5 4 3 2 1

Diagram A9

19

Chords in DADGAD Tuning

Key: ◯ Hold down the string at this fret ⊗ Don't play this string ◇ Optional fingering

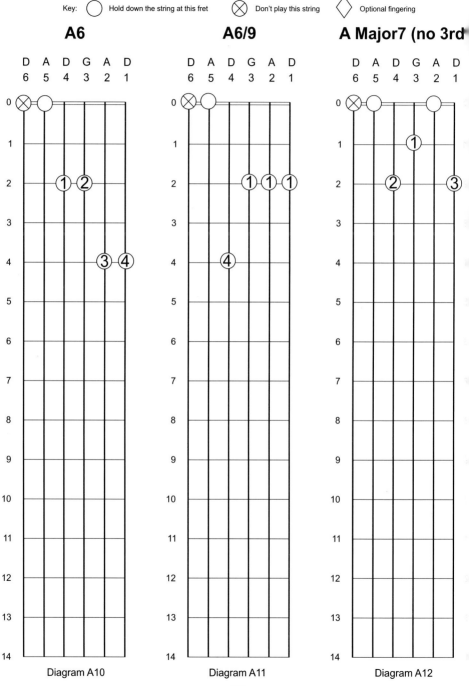

A6

A6/9

A Major7 (no 3rd)

Diagram A10

Diagram A11

Diagram A12

Chords in DADGAD Tuning

Key: ◯ Hold down the string at this fret ⊗ Don't play this string ◇ Optional fingering

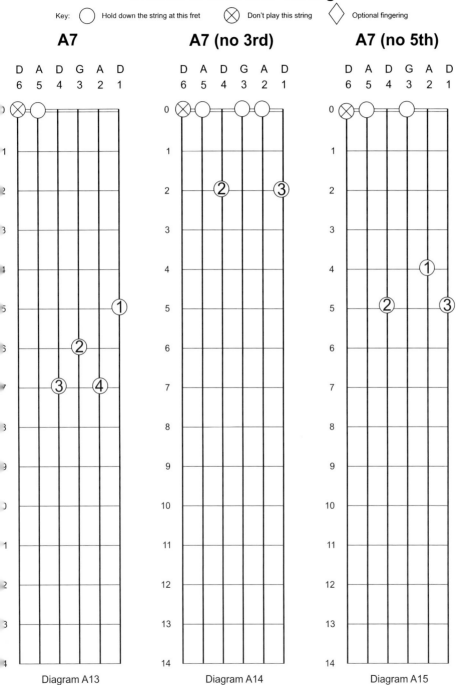

A7

A7 (no 3rd)

A7 (no 5th)

Diagram A13

Diagram A14

Diagram A15

21

Chords in DADGAD Tuning

Key: ◯ Hold down the string at this fret ⊗ Don't play this string ◇ Optional fingering

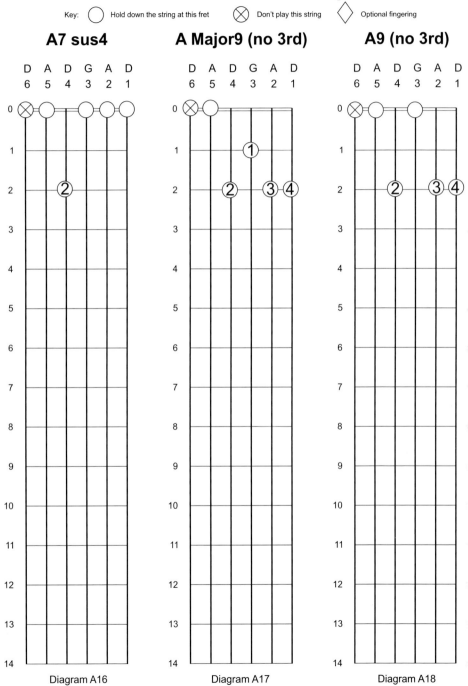

Diagram A16

Diagram A17

Diagram A18

22

Chords in DADGAD Tuning

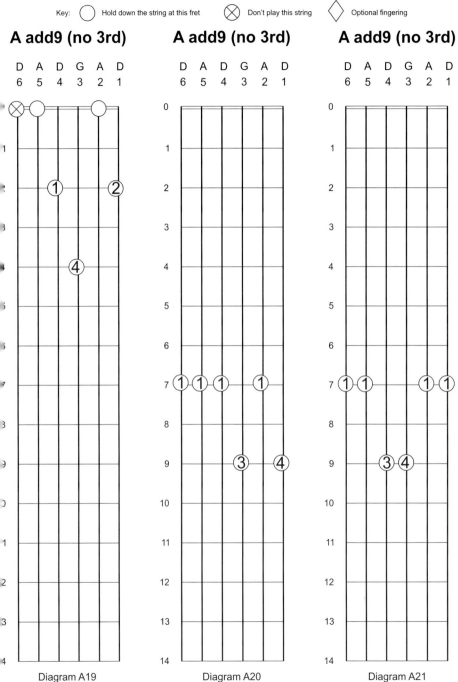

Diagram A19

Diagram A20

Diagram A21

23

Chords in DADGAD Tuning

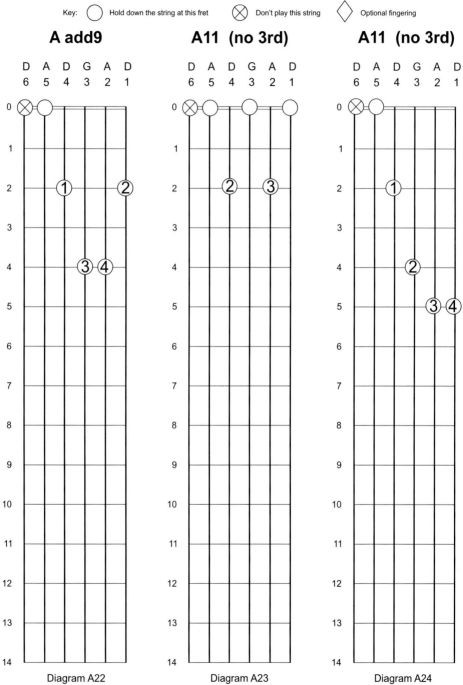

Chords in DADGAD Tuning

Key: ◯ Hold down the string at this fret   ⊗ Don't play this string   ◇ Optional fingering

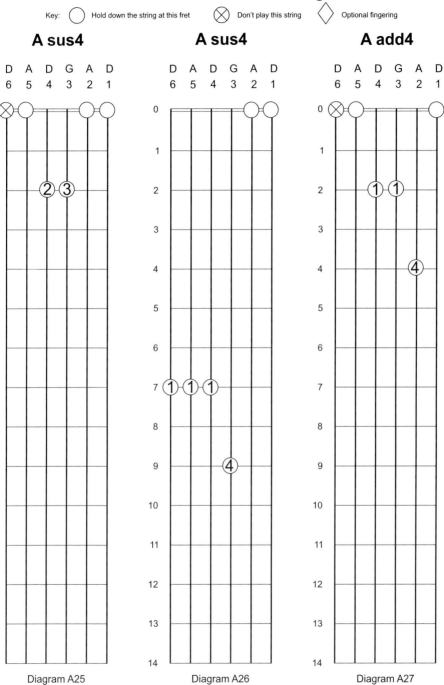

Diagram A25 — A sus4

Diagram A26 — A sus4

Diagram A27 — A add4

25

Chords in DADGAD Tuning

Key: ◯ Hold down the string at this fret   ⊗ Don't play this string   ◇ Optional fingering

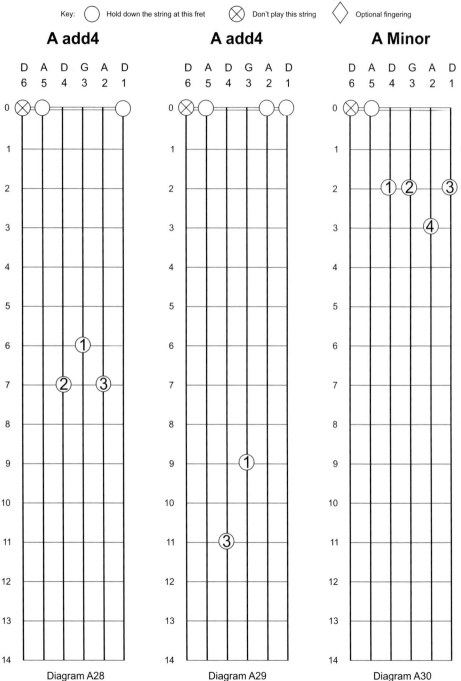

A add4

A add4

A Minor

Diagram A28   Diagram A29   Diagram A30

Chords in DADGAD Tuning

Key: ◯ Hold down the string at this fret   ⊗ Don't play this string   ◇ Optional fingering

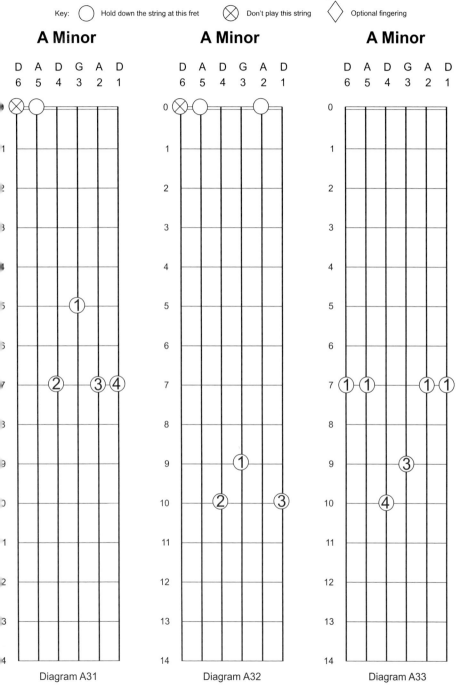

Diagram A31

Diagram A32

Diagram A33

27

Chords in DADGAD Tuning

Key: ◯ Hold down the string at this fret ⊗ Don't play this string ◇ Optional fingering

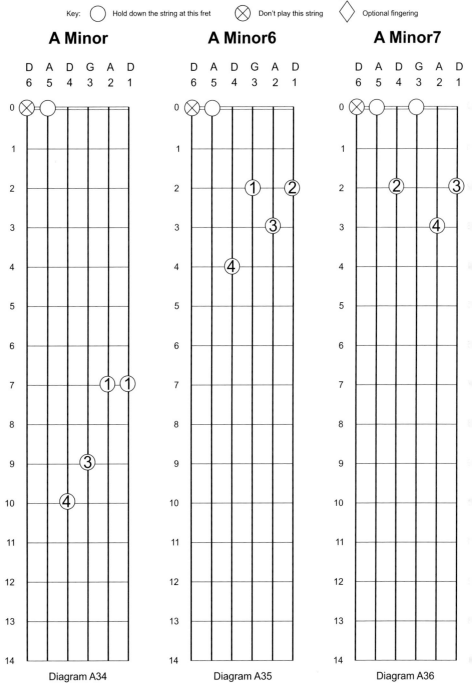

A Minor

Diagram A34

A Minor6

Diagram A35

A Minor7

Diagram A36

28

Chords in DADGAD Tuning

Key: Hold down the string at this fret · Don't play this string · Optional fingering

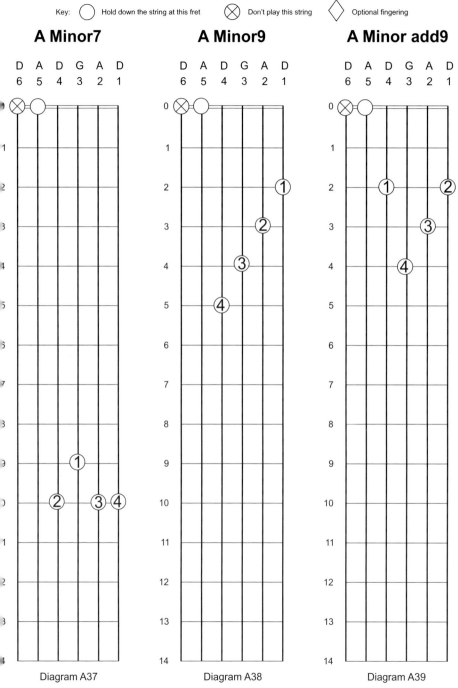

A Minor7
Diagram A37

A Minor9
Diagram A38

A Minor add9
Diagram A39

29

Chords in DADGAD Tuning

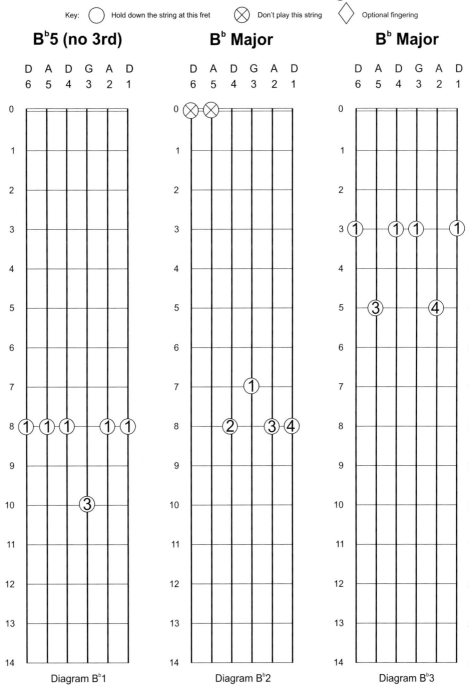

Diagram Bb1

Diagram Bb2

Diagram Bb3

Chords in DADGAD Tuning

Key: ⃝ Hold down the string at this fret ⊗ Don't play this string ◇ Optional fingering

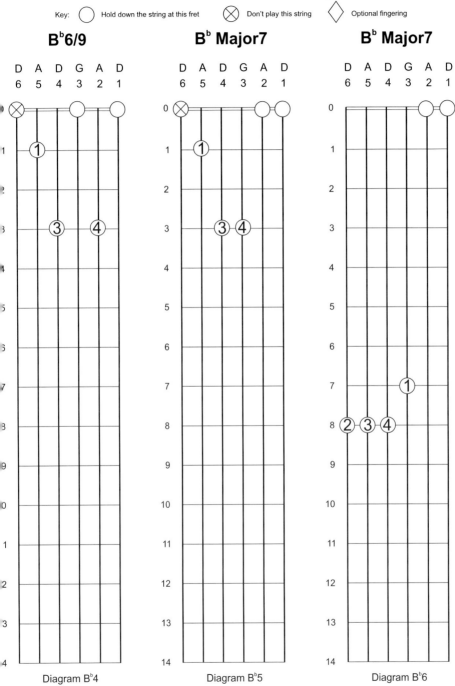

B♭6/9

B♭ Major7

B♭ Major7

Diagram B♭4

Diagram B♭5

Diagram B♭6

Chords in DADGAD Tuning

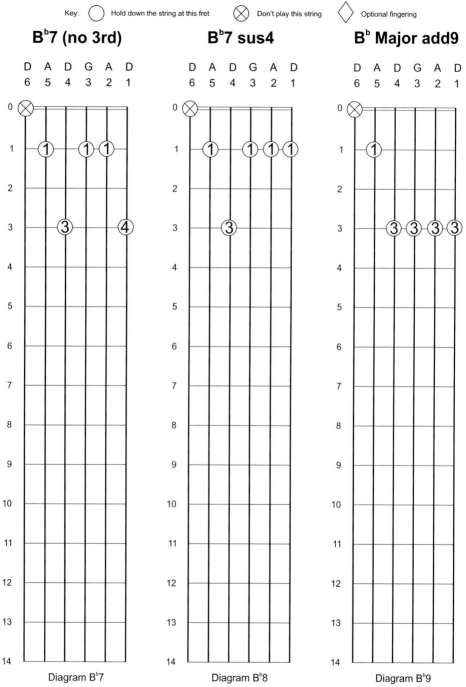

B♭7 (no 3rd)

Diagram B♭7

B♭7 sus4

Diagram B♭8

B♭ Major add9

Diagram B♭9

Chords in DADGAD Tuning

Key: ⭕ Hold down the string at this fret ⊗ Don't play this string ◇ Optional fingering

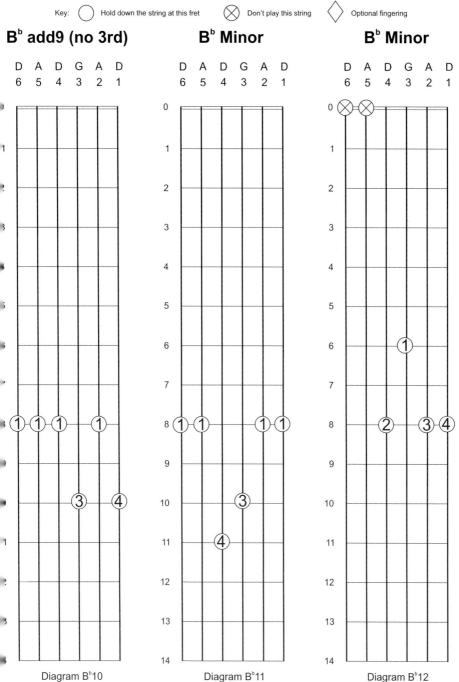

B♭ add9 (no 3rd) — Diagram B♭10

B♭ Minor — Diagram B♭11

B♭ Minor — Diagram B♭12

Chords in DADGAD Tuning

Key: ( ) Hold down the string at this fret ⊗ Don't play this string ◇ Optional fingering

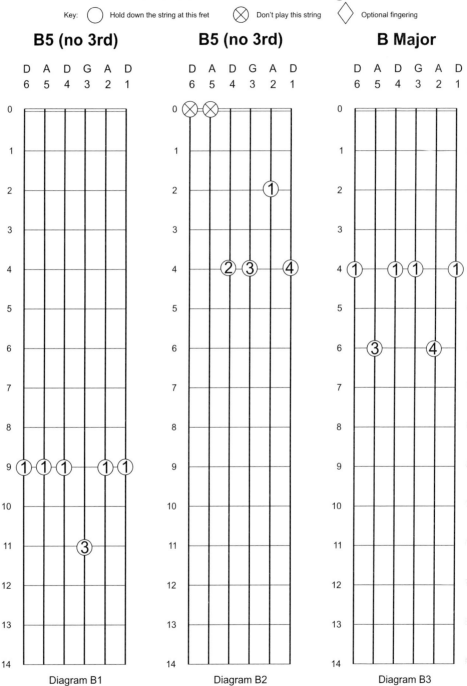

B5 (no 3rd)
Diagram B1

B5 (no 3rd)
Diagram B2

B Major
Diagram B3

Chords in DADGAD Tuning

Key: ◯ Hold down the string at this fret ⊗ Don't play this string ◇ Optional fingering

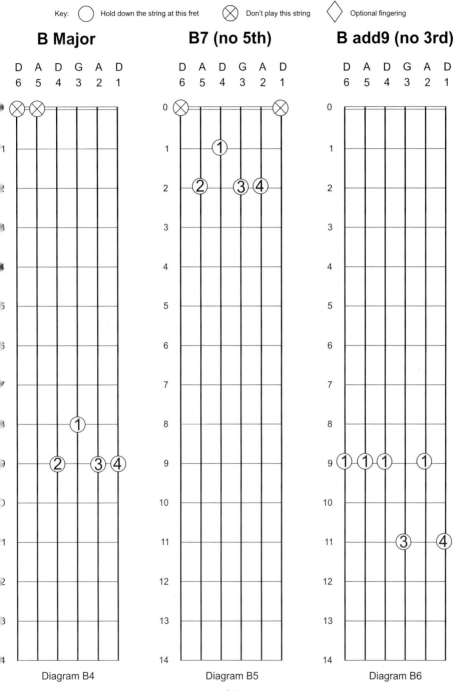

B Major

D	A	D	G	A	D
6	5	4	3	2	1

Diagram B4

B7 (no 5th)

D	A	D	G	A	D
6	5	4	3	2	1

Diagram B5

B add9 (no 3rd)

D	A	D	G	A	D
6	5	4	3	2	1

Diagram B6

35

Chords in DADGAD Tuning

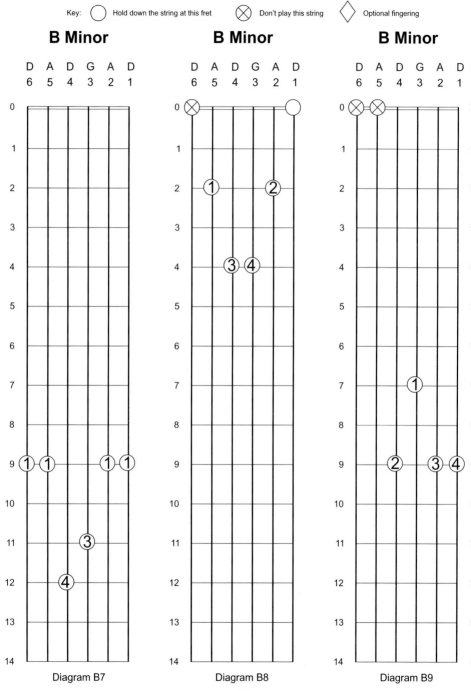

Chords in DADGAD Tuning

Key: ◯ Hold down the string at this fret   ⊗ Don't play this string   ◇ Optional fingering

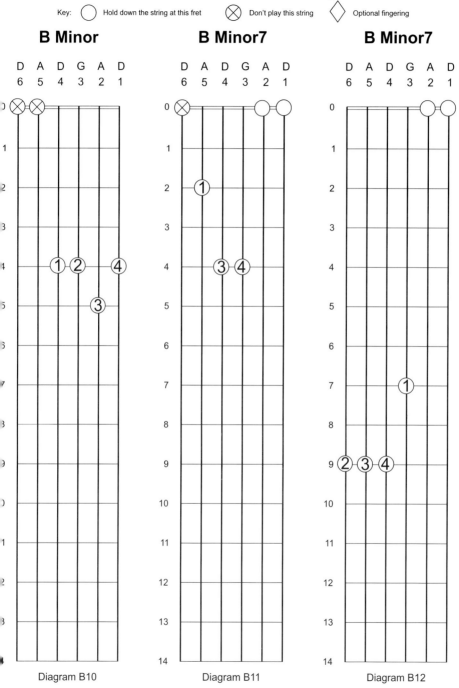

B Minor

Diagram B10

B Minor7

Diagram B11

B Minor7

Diagram B12

37

Chords in DADGAD Tuning

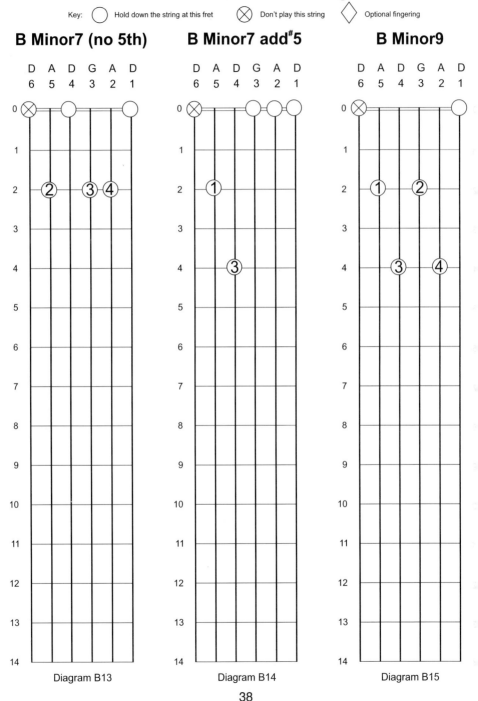

Key: ( ) Hold down the string at this fret   (X) Don't play this string   ◇ Optional fingering

B Minor7 (no 5th)

Diagram B13

B Minor7 add#5

Diagram B14

B Minor9

Diagram B15

38

Chords in DADGAD Tuning

Key: ◯ Hold down the string at this fret   ⊗ Don't play this string   ◇ Optional fingering

B Minor9

B Minor add9

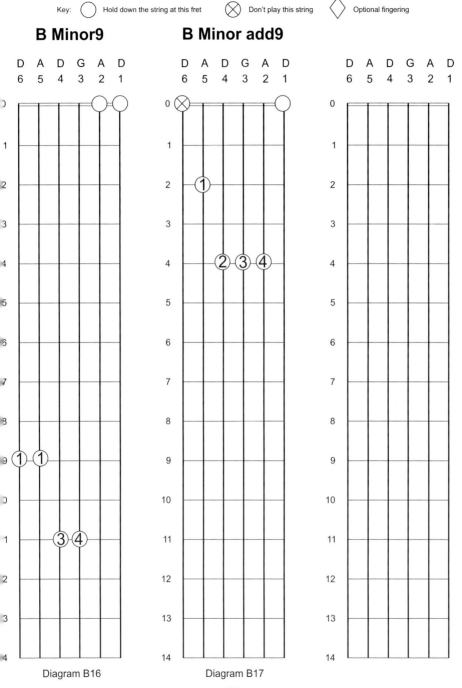

Diagram B16

Diagram B17

39

Chords in DADGAD Tuning

Key: ◯ Hold down the string at this fret   ⊗ Don't play this string   ◇ Optional fingering

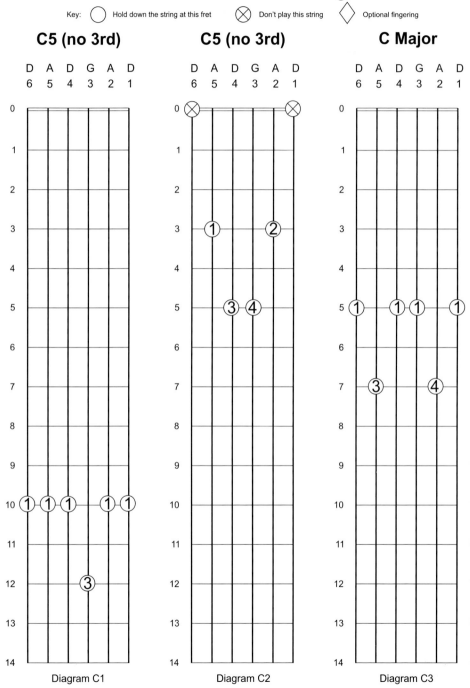

C5 (no 3rd) — Diagram C1

C5 (no 3rd) — Diagram C2

C Major — Diagram C3

40

Chords in DADGAD Tuning

Key: ◯ Hold down the string at this fret   ⊗ Don't play this string   ◇ Optional fingering

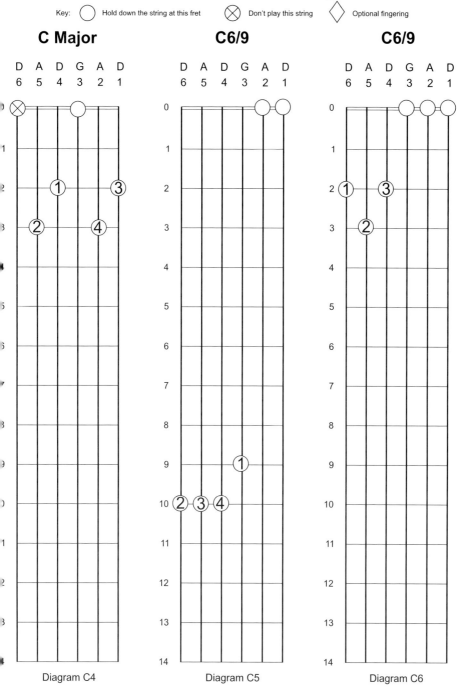

C Major

Diagram C4

C6/9

Diagram C5

C6/9

Diagram C6

41

Chords in DADGAD Tuning

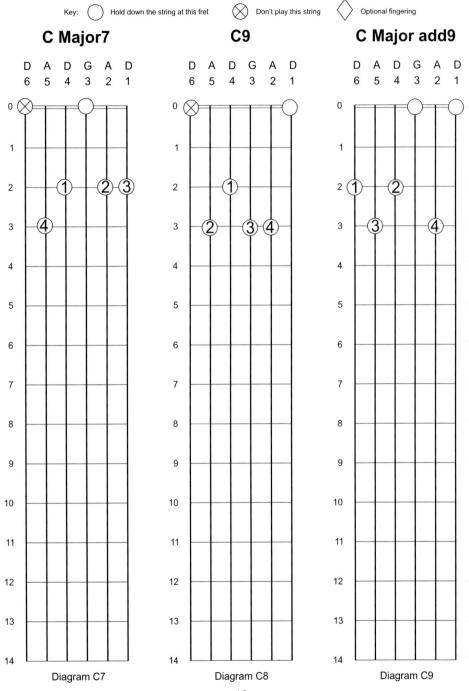

Key: ◯ Hold down the string at this fret   ⊗ Don't play this string   ◇ Optional fingering

C Major7

D	A	D	G	A	D
6	5	4	3	2	1

Diagram C7

C9

D	A	D	G	A	D
6	5	4	3	2	1

Diagram C8

C Major add9

D	A	D	G	A	D
6	5	4	3	2	1

Diagram C9

42

Chords in DADGAD Tuning

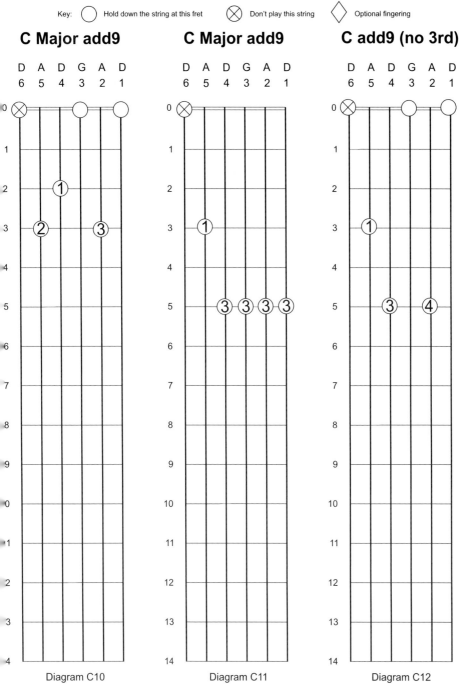

C Major add9
Diagram C10

C Major add9
Diagram C11

C add9 (no 3rd)
Diagram C12

Chords in DADGAD Tuning

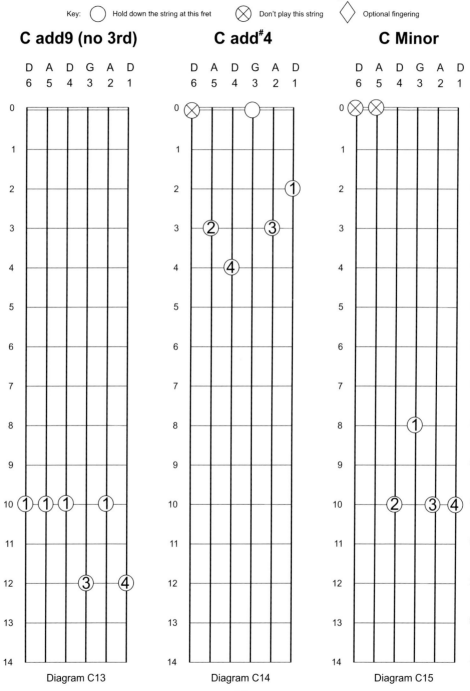

C add9 (no 3rd)

Diagram C13

C add#4

Diagram C14

C Minor

Diagram C15

44

Chords in DADGAD Tuning

Key: ◯ Hold down the string at this fret   ⊗ Don't play this string   ◇ Optional fingering

C Minor

C Minor add9

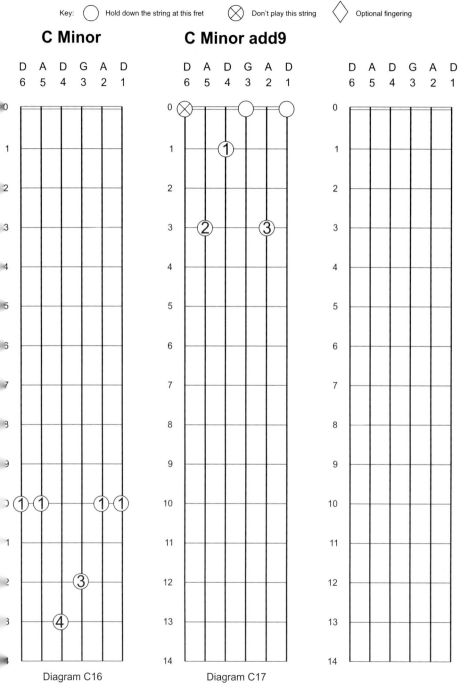

Diagram C16

Diagram C17

Chords in DADGAD Tuning

Key: ◯ Hold down the string at this fret ⊗ Don't play this string ◇ Optional fingering

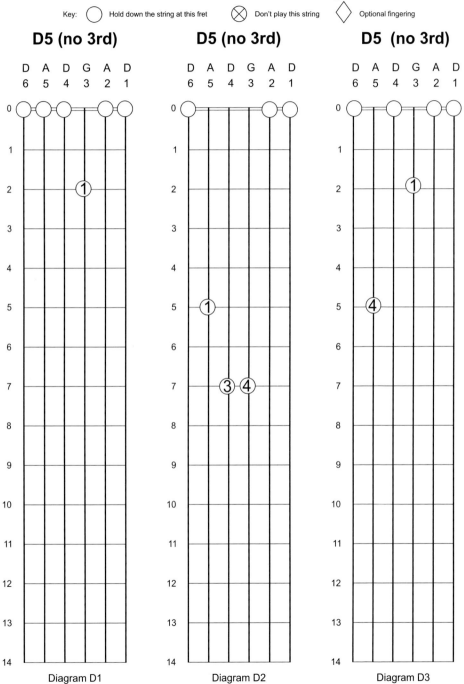

Diagram D1 Diagram D2 Diagram D3

46

Chords in DADGAD Tuning

Key: ( ) Hold down the string at this fret   ⊗ Don't play this string   ◇ Optional fingering

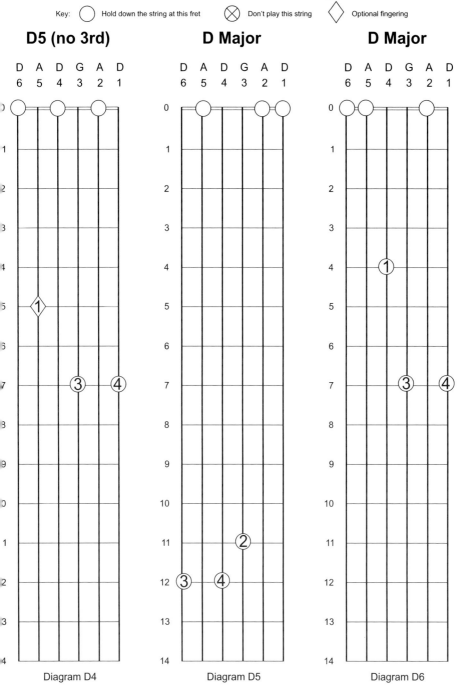

D5 (no 3rd)

Diagram D4

D Major

Diagram D5

D Major

Diagram D6

47

Chords in DADGAD Tuning

Key: ◯ Hold down the string at this fret   ⊗ Don't play this string   ◇ Optional fingering

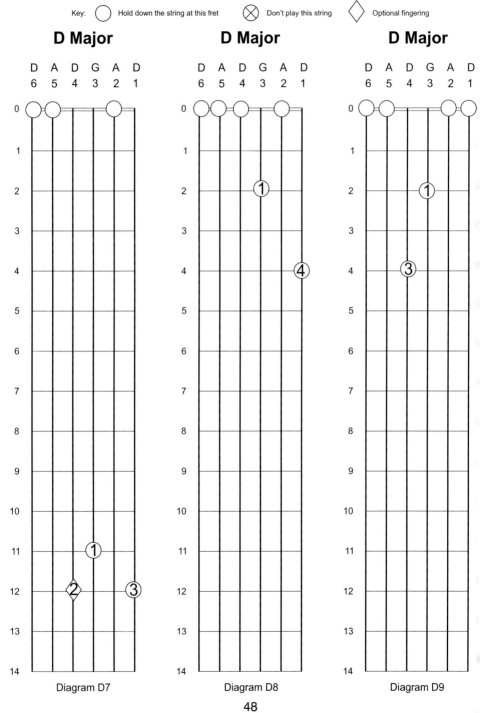

D Major

D	A	D	G	A	D
6	5	4	3	2	1

Diagram D7

D Major

D	A	D	G	A	D
6	5	4	3	2	1

Diagram D8

D Major

D	A	D	G	A	D
6	5	4	3	2	1

Diagram D9

Chords in DADGAD Tuning

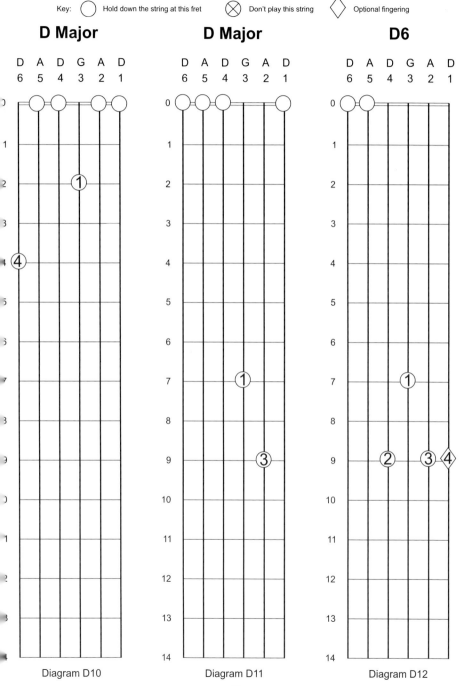

Diagram D10

Diagram D11

Diagram D12

Chords in DADGAD Tuning

Key: ◯ Hold down the string at this fret   ⊗ Don't play this string   ◇ Optional fingering

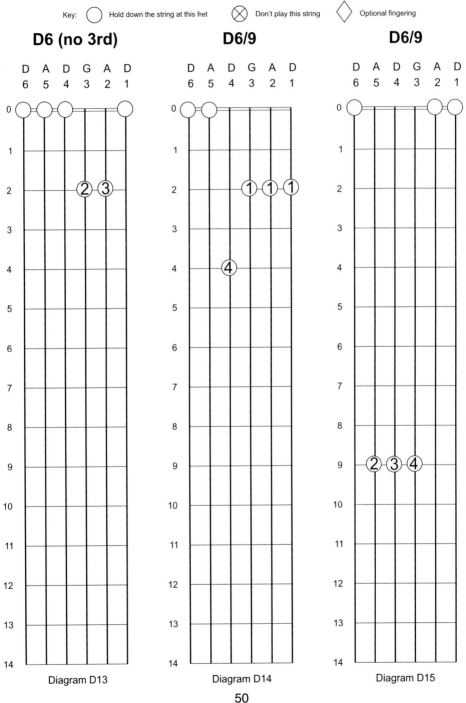

D6 (no 3rd)
Diagram D13

D6/9
Diagram D14

D6/9
Diagram D15

50

Chords in DADGAD Tuning

Key: ◯ Hold down the string at this fret   ⊗ Don't play this string   ◇ Optional fingering

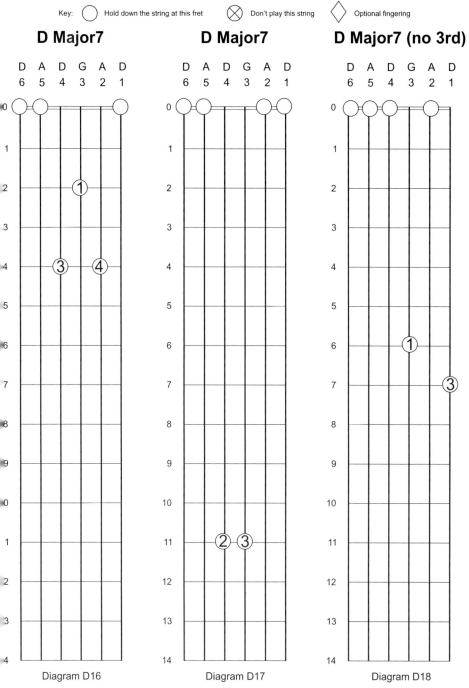

D Major7

Diagram D16

D Major7

Diagram D17

D Major7 (no 3rd)

Diagram D18

51

Chords in DADGAD Tuning

Key: ◯ Hold down the string at this fret   ⊗ Don't play this string   ◇ Optional fingering

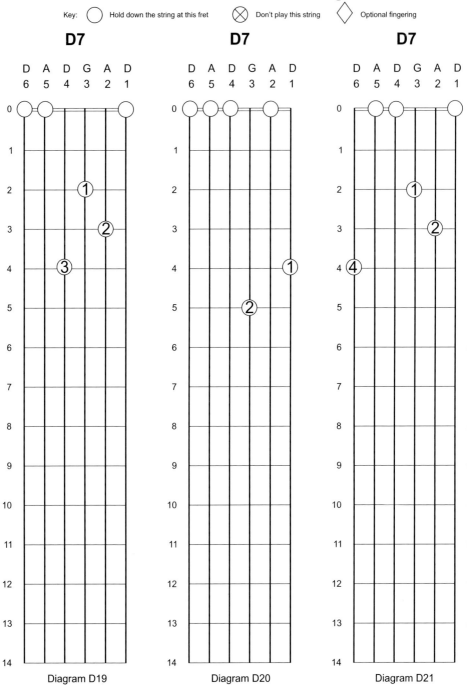

D7	D7	D7

Diagram D19   Diagram D20   Diagram D21

Chords in DADGAD Tuning

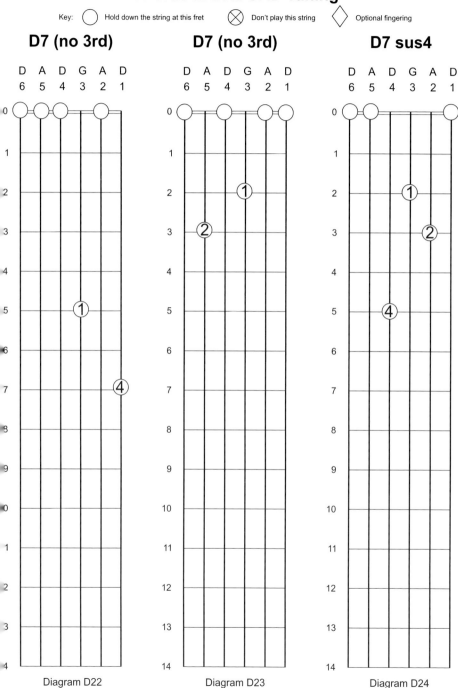

D7 (no 3rd)

Diagram D22

D7 (no 3rd)

Diagram D23

D7 sus4

Diagram D24

53

Chords in DADGAD Tuning

Key: ⭕ Hold down the string at this fret   ⊗ Don't play this string   ◇ Optional fingering

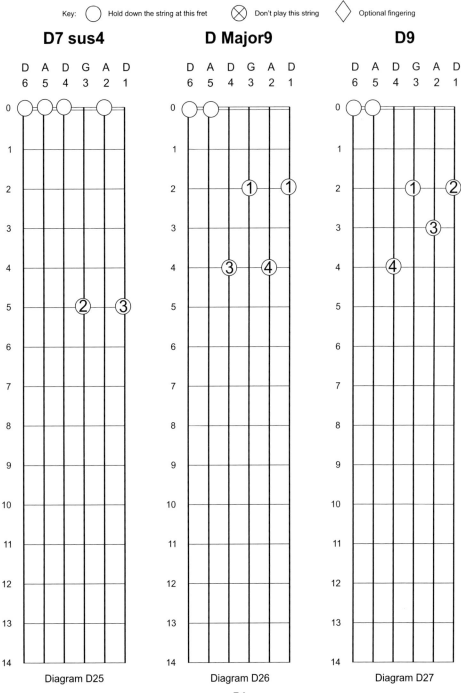

D7 sus4

Diagram D25

D Major9

Diagram D26

D9

Diagram D27

54

Chords in DADGAD Tuning

Key: ( ) Hold down the string at this fret   (⊗) Don't play this string   (◇) Optional fingering

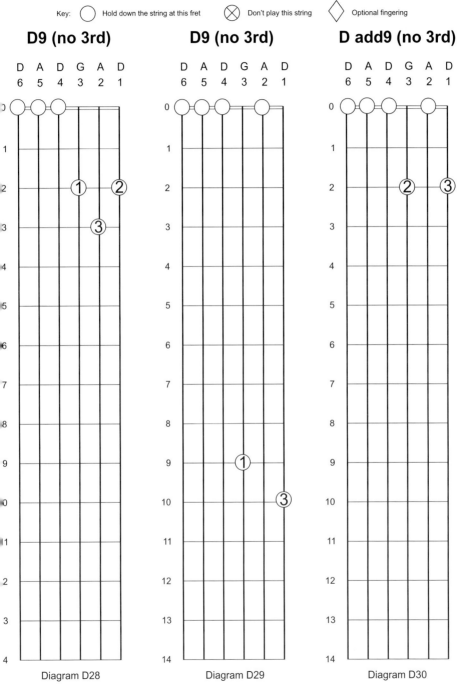

D9 (no 3rd)

D	A	D	G	A	D
6	5	4	3	2	1

Diagram D28

D9 (no 3rd)

D	A	D	G	A	D
6	5	4	3	2	1

Diagram D29

D add9 (no 3rd)

D	A	D	G	A	D
6	5	4	3	2	1

Diagram D30

55

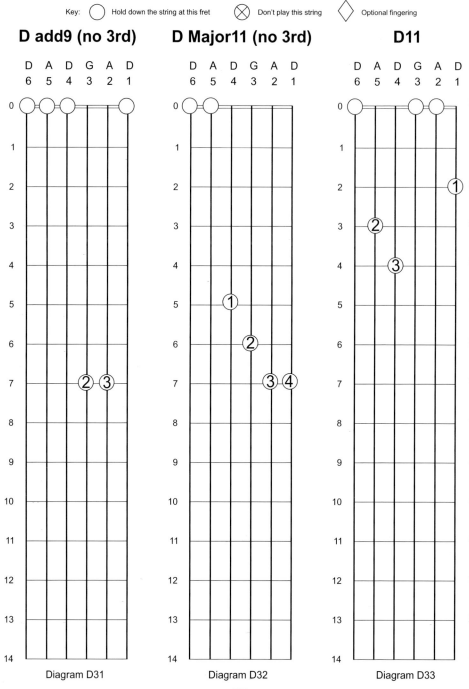

Key: ◯ Hold down the string at this fret   ⊗ Don't play this string   ◇ Optional fingering

D add9 (no 3rd)   D Major11 (no 3rd)   D11

Diagram D31   Diagram D32   Diagram D33

Chords in DADGAD Tuning

Key: ◯ Hold down the string at this fret   ⊗ Don't play this string   ◇ Optional fingering

D11 (no 3rd)   D11 (no 3rd)   D11 (no 3rd)

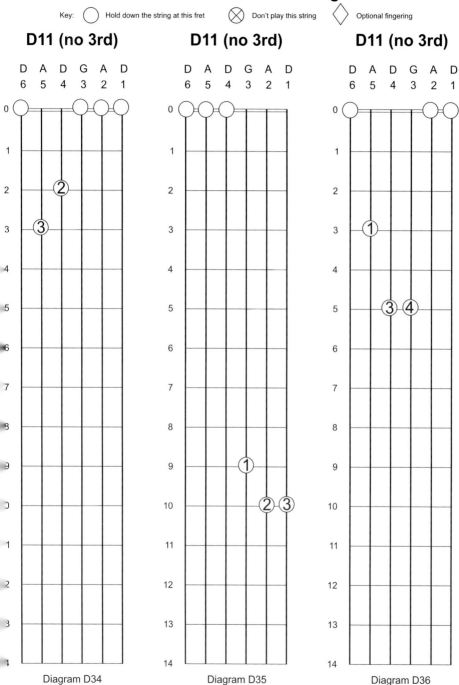

Diagram D34   Diagram D35   Diagram D36

57

Chords in DADGAD Tuning

Key: ◯ Hold down the string at this fret   ⊗ Don't play this string   ◇ Optional fingering

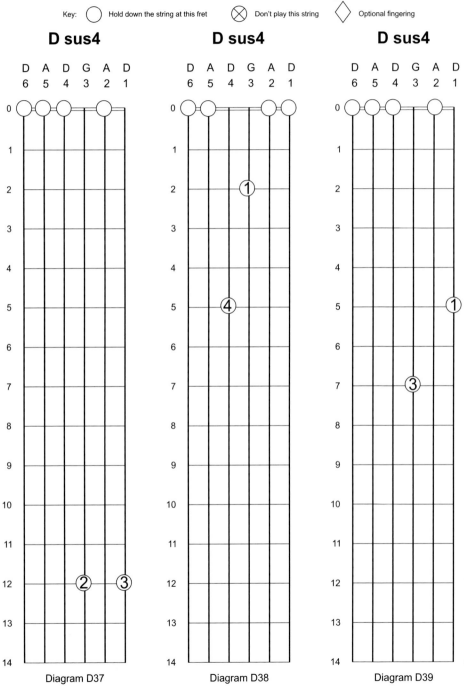

D sus4

D sus4

D sus4

Diagram D37

Diagram D38

Diagram D39

58

Chords in DADGAD Tuning

Key: ◯ Hold down the string at this fret ⊗ Don't play this string ◇ Optional fingering

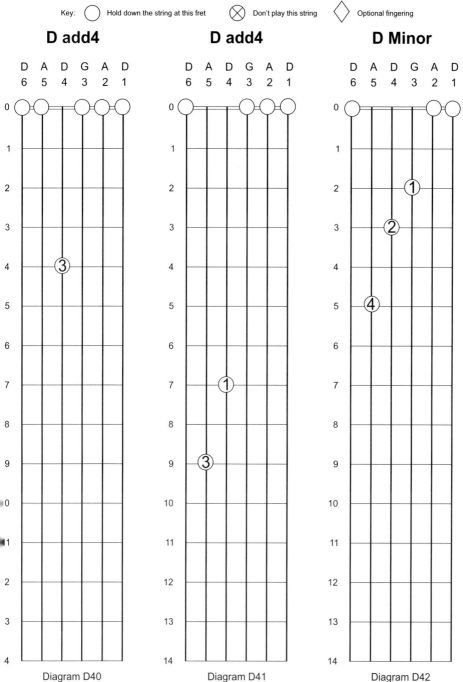

Diagram D40   Diagram D41   Diagram D42

Chords in DADGAD Tuning

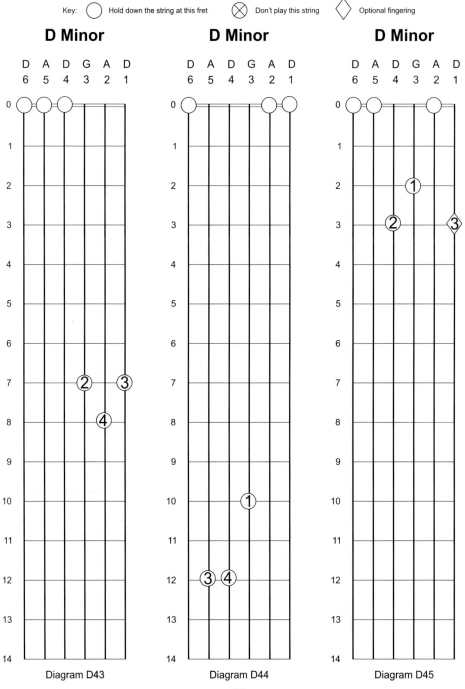

D Minor
Diagram D43

D Minor
Diagram D44

D Minor
Diagram D45

Chords in DADGAD Tuning

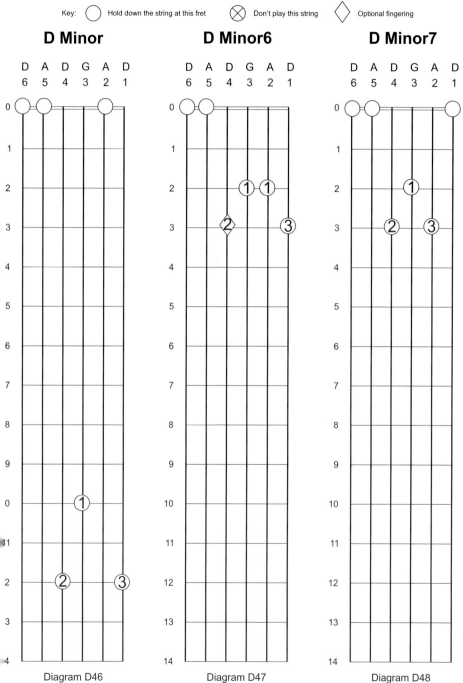

D Minor

D Minor6

D Minor7

Diagram D46

Diagram D47

Diagram D48

Chords in DADGAD Tuning

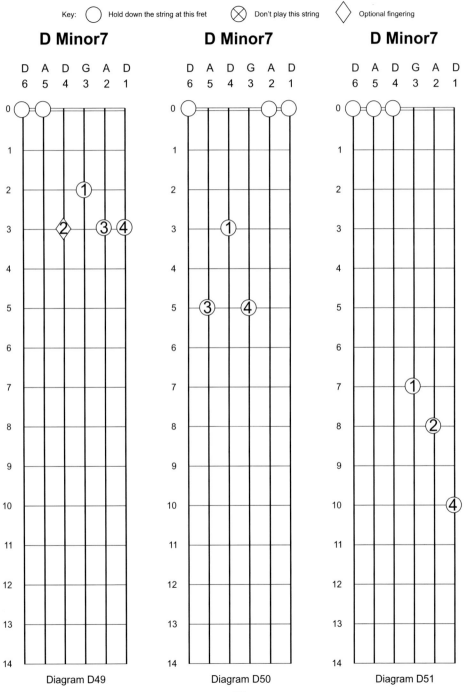

D Minor7	D Minor7	D Minor7
Diagram D49	Diagram D50	Diagram D51

Chords in DADGAD Tuning

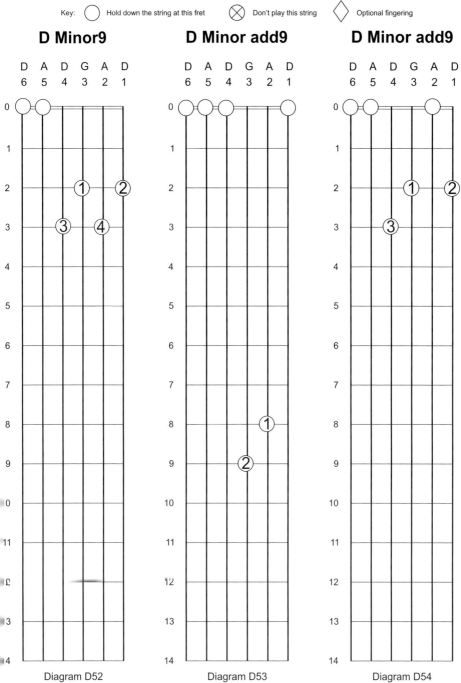

D Minor9

D	A	D	G	A	D
6	5	4	3	2	1

Diagram D52

D Minor add9

D	A	D	G	A	D
6	5	4	3	2	1

Diagram D53

D Minor add9

D	A	D	G	A	D
6	5	4	3	2	1

Diagram D54

63

Chords in DADGAD Tuning

D Minor11

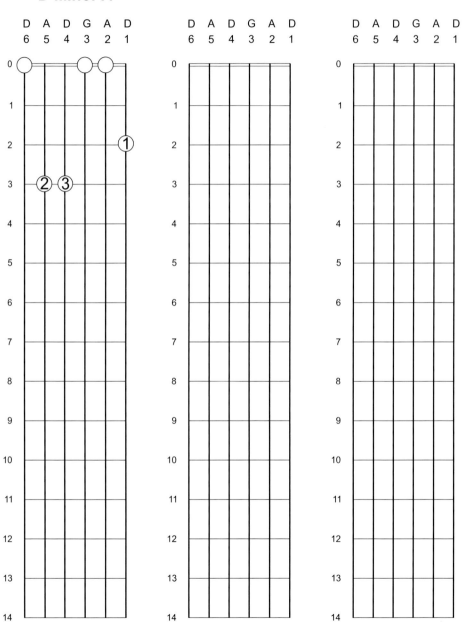

Diagram D55

Chords in DADGAD Tuning

Key: ◯ Hold down the string at this fret   ⊗ Don't play this string   ◇ Optional fingering

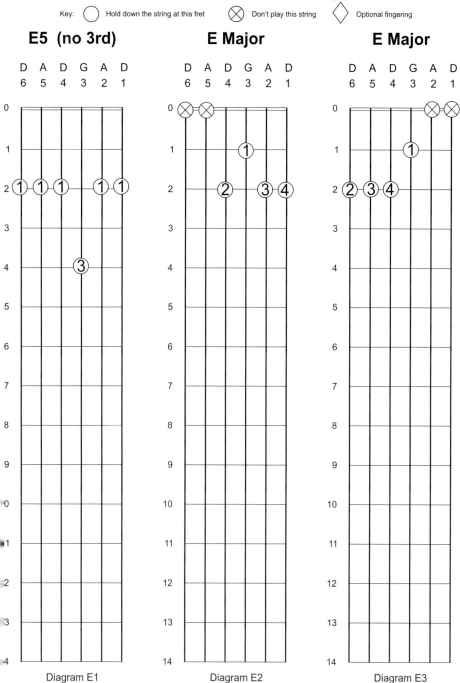

E5 (no 3rd)   E Major   E Major

Diagram E1   Diagram E2   Diagram E3

65

Chords in DADGAD Tuning

Key: ◯ Hold down the string at this fret   ⊗ Don't play this string   ◇ Optional fingering

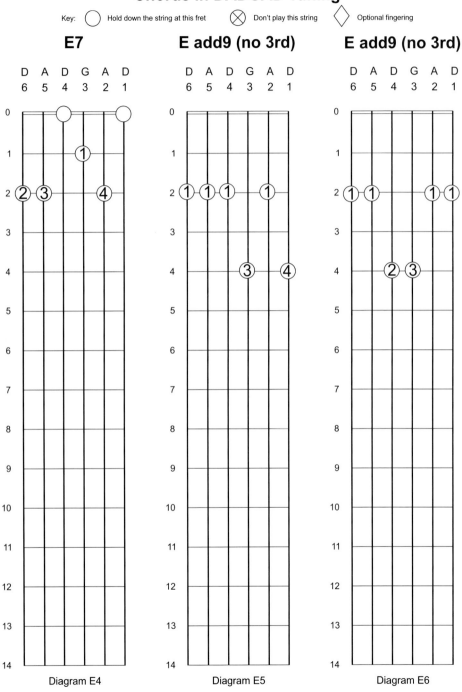

E7

D	A	D	G	A	D
6	5	4	3	2	1

Diagram E4

E add9 (no 3rd)

D	A	D	G	A	D
6	5	4	3	2	1

Diagram E5

E add9 (no 3rd)

D	A	D	G	A	D
6	5	4	3	2	1

Diagram E6

66

Chords in DADGAD Tuning

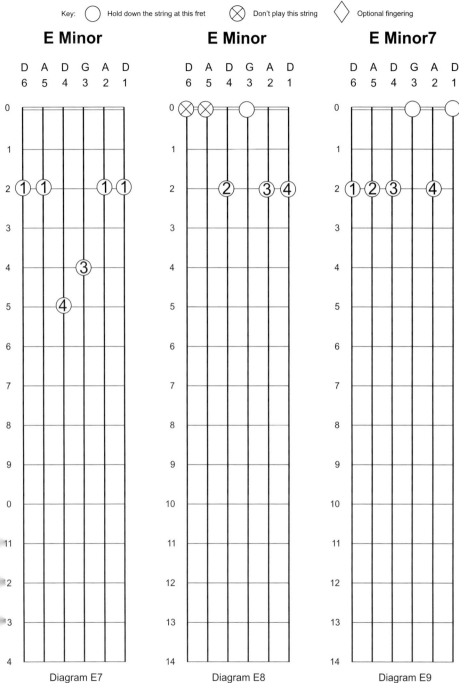

Key: ◯ Hold down the string at this fret   ⊗ Don't play this string   ◇ Optional fingering

E Minor   E Minor   E Minor7

Diagram E7

Diagram E8

Diagram E9

67

Chords in DADGAD Tuning

Key: ◯ Hold down the string at this fret ⊗ Don't play this string ◇ Optional fingering

E Minor11

D	A	D	G	A	D
6	5	4	3	2	1

Diagram E10

E Minor11 (no 9th)

D	A	D	G	A	D
6	5	4	3	2	1

Diagram E11

D	A	D	G	A	D
6	5	4	3	2	1

Chords in DADGAD Tuning

Key: ◯ Hold down the string at this fret   ⊗ Don't play this string   ◇ Optional fingering

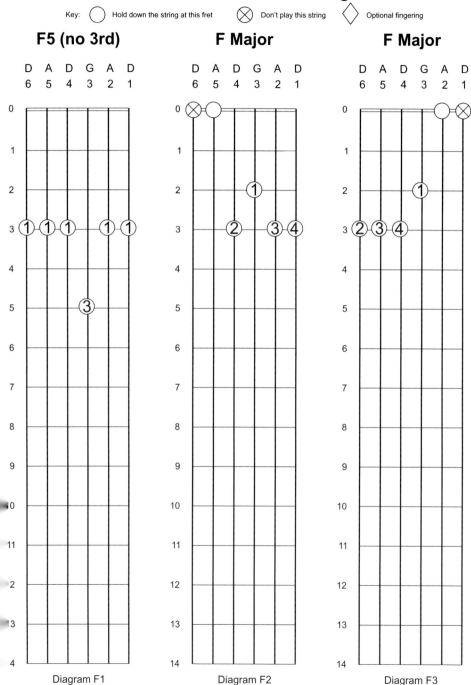

F5 (no 3rd)

Diagram F1

F Major

Diagram F2

F Major

Diagram F3

Chords in DADGAD Tuning

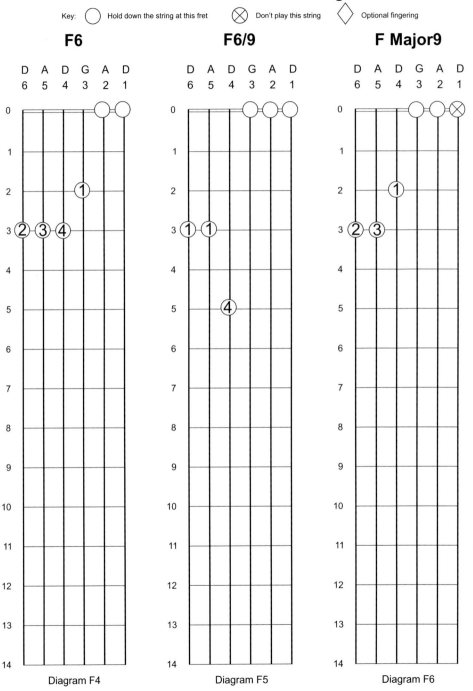

F6

Diagram F4

F6/9

Diagram F5

F Major9

Diagram F6

70

Chords in DADGAD Tuning

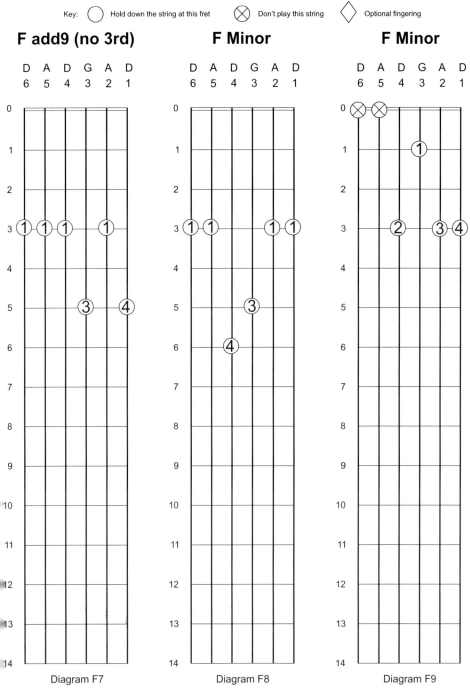

Key: ◯ Hold down the string at this fret   ⊗ Don't play this string   ◇ Optional fingering

F add9 (no 3rd)

F Minor

F Minor

Diagram F7

Diagram F8

Diagram F9

Chords in DADGAD Tuning

Key: ( ) Hold down the string at this fret   ⊗ Don't play this string   ◇ Optional fingering

F Minor

```
D   A   D   G   A   D
6   5   4   3   2   1
```

Diagram F10

F Minor6

```
D   A   D   G   A   D
6   5   4   3   2   1
```

Diagram F11

```
D   A   D   G   A   D
6   5   4   3   2   1
```

72

Chords in DADGAD Tuning

Key: ◯ Hold down the string at this fret   ⊗ Don't play this string   ◇ Optional fingering

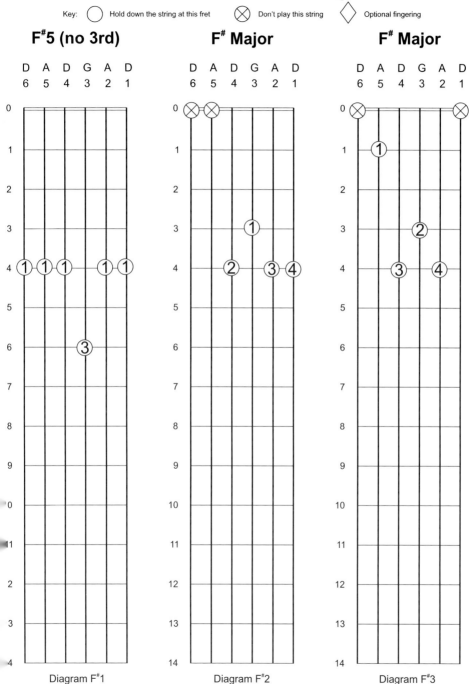

Diagram F#1   Diagram F#2   Diagram F#3

73

Chords in DADGAD Tuning

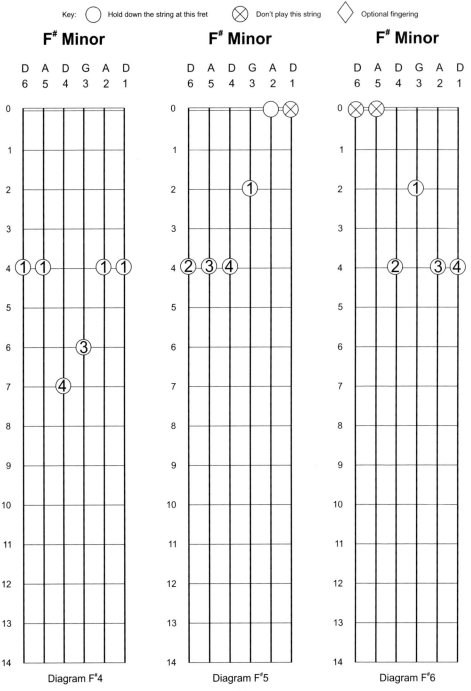

Key: ( ) Hold down the string at this fret   (⊗) Don't play this string   ◇ Optional fingering

Diagram F#4

Diagram F#5

Diagram F#6

74

Chords in DADGAD Tuning

F# add9 (no 3rd)

D	A	D	G	A	D
6	5	4	3	2	1

Diagram F#7

F# add9 (no 3rd)

D	A	D	G	A	D
6	5	4	3	2	1

Diagram F#8

D	A	D	G	A	D
6	5	4	3	2	1

75

Chords in DADGAD Tuning

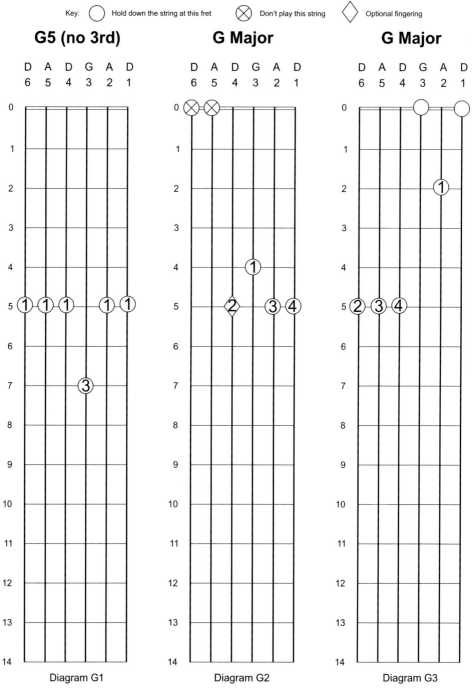

Chords in DADGAD Tuning

Key: ◯ Hold down the string at this fret   ⊗ Don't play this string   ◇ Optional fingering

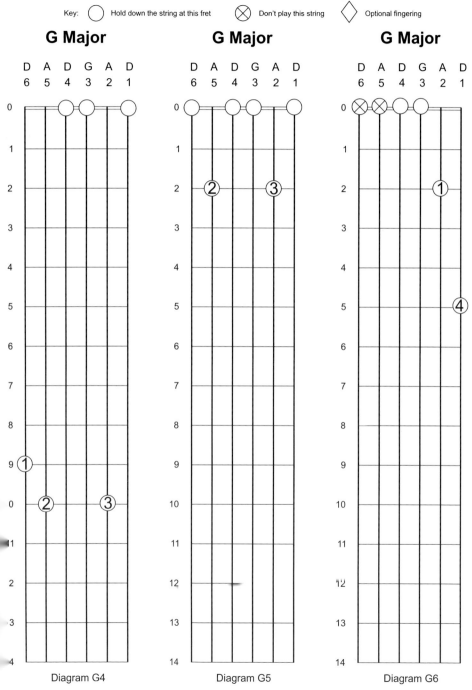

G Major
Diagram G4

G Major
Diagram G5

G Major
Diagram G6

Chords in DADGAD Tuning

Key: ◯ Hold down the string at this fret ⊗ Don't play this string ◇ Optional fingering

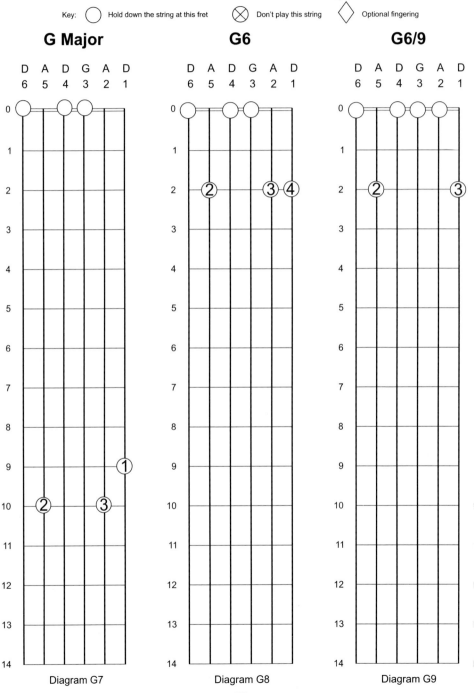

G Major

Diagram G7

G6

Diagram G8

G6/9

Diagram G9

78

Chords in DADGAD Tuning

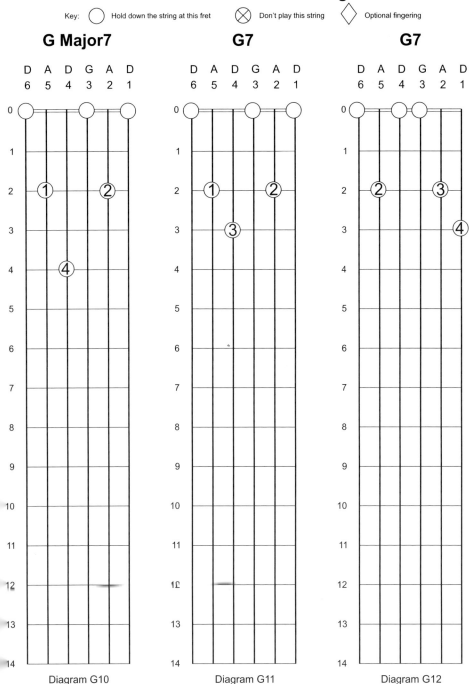

G Major7

G7

G7

Diagram G10

Diagram G11

Diagram G12

Chords in DADGAD Tuning

G Major add9

D	A	D	G	A	D
6	5	4	3	2	1

Diagram G13

G Major add9

D	A	D	G	A	D
6	5	4	3	2	1

Diagram G14

G add9 (no 3rd)

D	A	D	G	A	D
6	5	4	3	2	1

Diagram G15

80

Chords in DADGAD Tuning

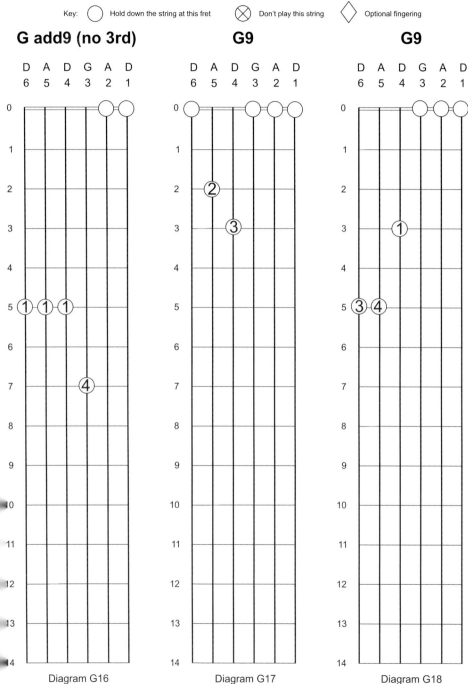

G add9 (no 3rd)   G9   G9

Diagram G16   Diagram G17   Diagram G18

Chords in DADGAD Tuning

Key: ◯ Hold down the string at this fret   ⊗ Don't play this string   ◇ Optional fingering

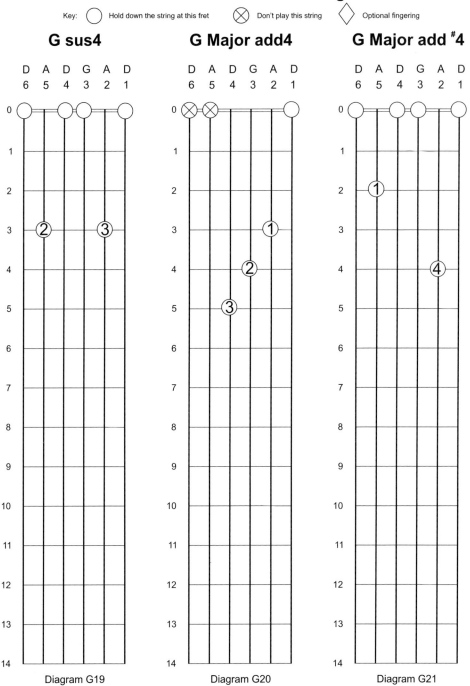

G sus4

Diagram G19

G Major add4

Diagram G20

G Major add #4

Diagram G21

82

Chords in DADGAD Tuning

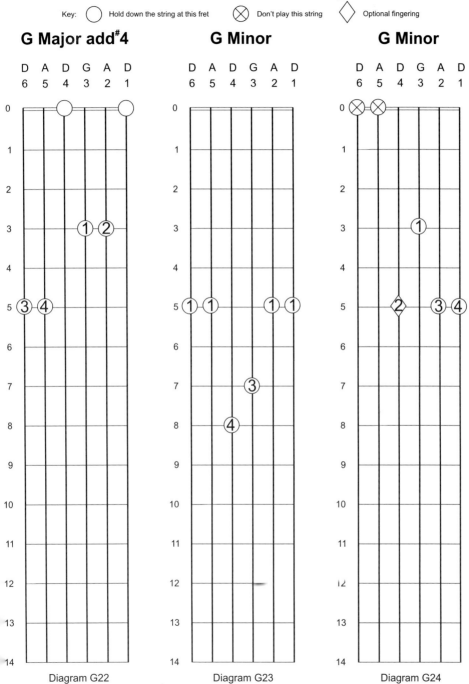

Key: ◯ Hold down the string at this fret   ⊗ Don't play this string   ◇ Optional fingering

G Major add#4

G Minor

G Minor

Diagram G22

Diagram G23

Diagram G24

Chords in DADGAD Tuning

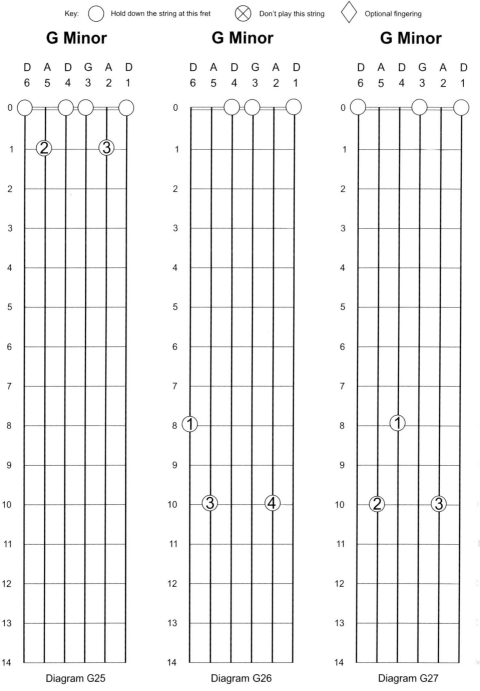

Key: ◯ Hold down the string at this fret   ⊗ Don't play this string   ◇ Optional fingering

G Minor

G Minor

G Minor

Diagram G25

Diagram G26

Diagram G27

Chords in DADGAD Tuning

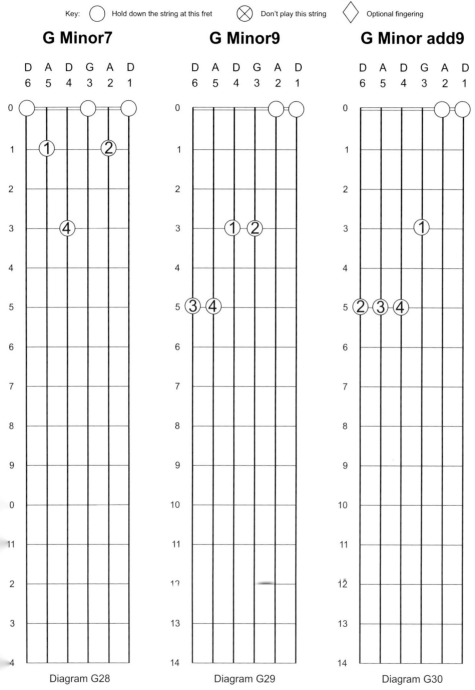

G Minor7

G Minor9

G Minor add9

Diagram G28

Diagram G29

Diagram G30

Chords in DADGAD Tuning

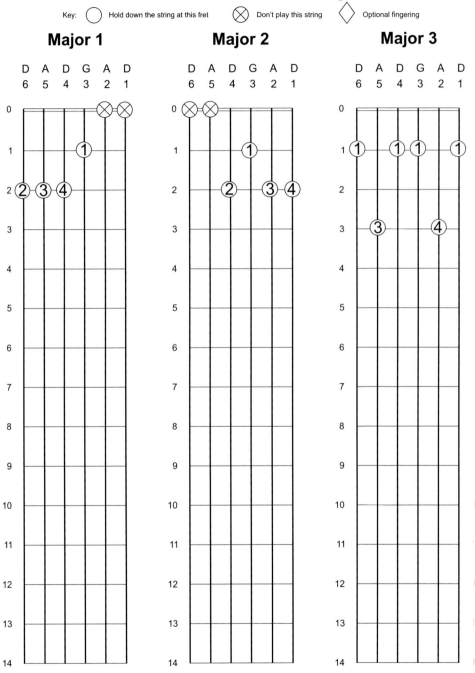

Key: ⊘ Hold down the string at this fret   ⊗ Don't play this string   ◇ Optional fingering

Major 1

Major 2

Major 3

Chords in DADGAD Tuning

Minor 1

D	A	D	G	A	D
6	5	4	3	2	1

Minor 2

D	A	D	G	A	D
6	5	4	3	2	1

Minor 3

D	A	D	G	A	D
6	5	4	3	2	1

87

Chords in DADGAD Tuning

Key: ◯ Hold down the string at this fret   ⊗ Don't play this string   ◇ Optional fingering

5 (no 3rd)

D	A	D	G	A	D
6	5	4	3	2	1

Add9 (no 3rd)

D	A	D	G	A	D
6	5	4	3	2	1

Major add9

D	A	D	G	A	D
6	5	4	3	2	1

Chords in DADGAD Tuning

Key: ◯ Hold down the string at this fret ⊗ Don't play this string ◇ Optional fingering

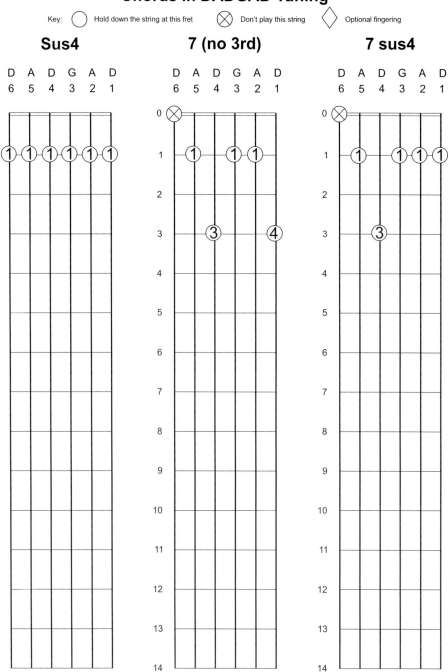

89

Chords in DADGAD Tuning

Key: ◯ Hold down the string at this fret ⊗ Don't play this string ◇ Optional fingering

Phrase 1A i

D	A	D	G	A	D
6	5	4	3	2	1

0 — ◯ (string 1)
2 — ① (string 1)
4 — ④ (string 1)

Phrase 1A iii

D	A	D	G	A	D
6	5	4	3	2	1

0 — ◯ ◯ ◯ (strings 3, 2, 1)
2 — ① (string 1)
4 — ③ (string 5) ④ (string 1)

Phrase 1B

D	A	D	G	A	D
6	5	4	3	2	1

0 — ◯ (string 1)
2 — ① (string 1)
4 — ④ (string 1)

90

Chords in DADGAD Tuning

Key: ◯ Hold down the string at this fret ⊗ Don't play this string ◇ Optional fingering

Phrase 1C

D	A	D	G	A	D
6	5	4	3	2	1

Phrase 2A

D	A	D	G	A	D
6	5	4	3	2	1

Phrase 2B

D	A	D	G	A	D
6	5	4	3	2	1

Chords in DADGAD Tuning

Key: ◯ Hold down the string at this fret   ⊗ Don't play this string   ◇ Optional fingering

Chord Diagrams for your use

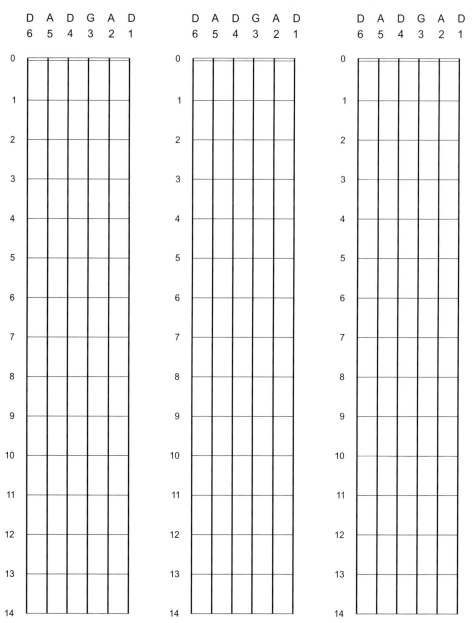

Chords in DADGAD Tuning

Key: ⭕ Hold down the string at this fret ⊗ Don't play this string ◇ Optional fingering

Chord Diagrams for your use

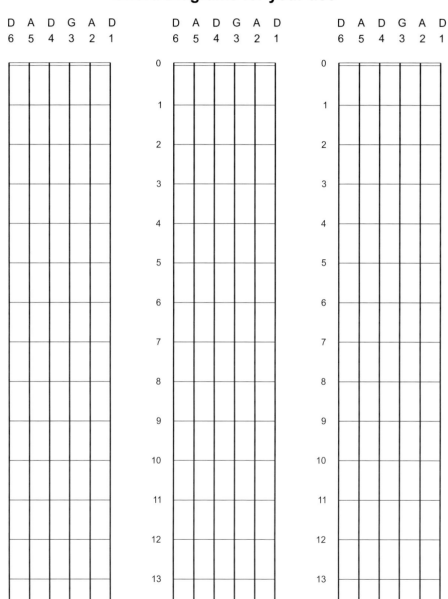

Chords in DADGAD Tuning

Key: ◯ Hold down the string at this fret ⊗ Don't play this string ◇ Optional fingering

Chord Diagrams for your use

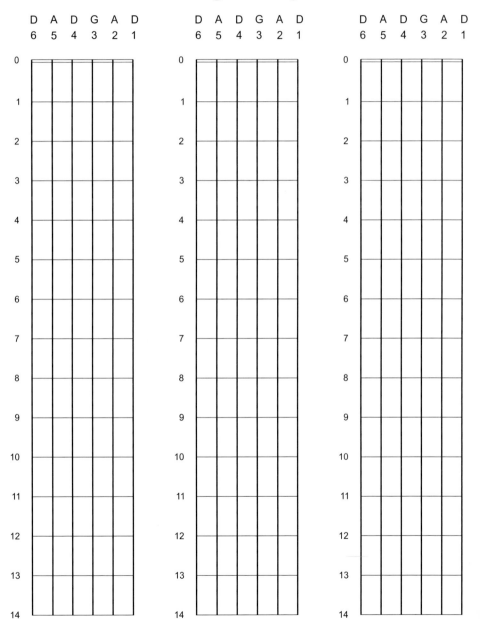

94

Chords in DADGAD Tuning

Key: ◯ Hold down the string at this fret   ⊗ Don't play this string   ◇ Optional fingering

Chord Diagrams for your use

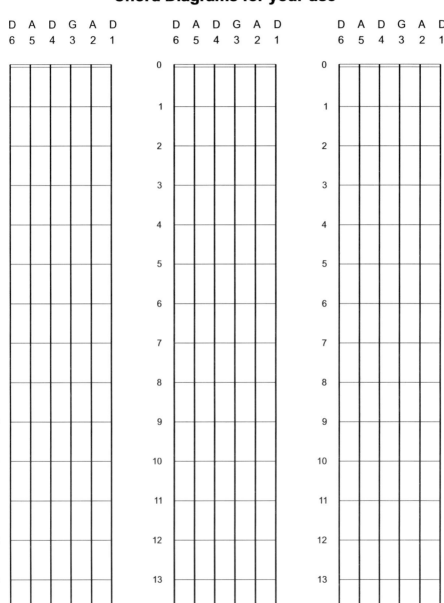

95

Chords in DADGAD Tuning

Key: ◯ Hold down the string at this fret   ⊗ Don't play this string   ◇ Optional fingering

Chord Diagrams for your use

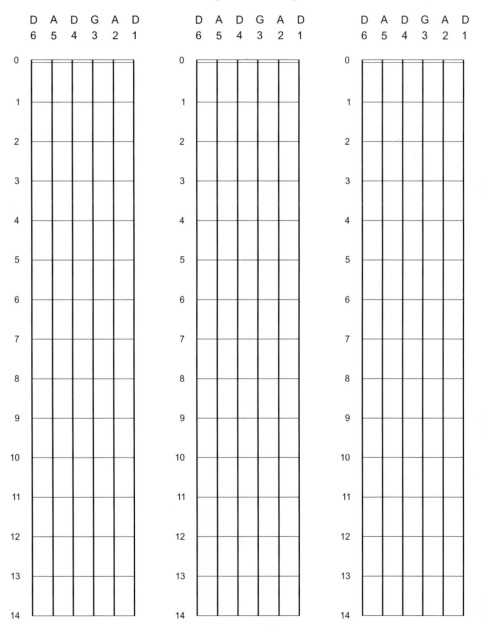